OXFORD REVISE

OCR GCSE

COMPUTER SCIENCE

COMPLETE REVISION AND PRACTICE

Alison Page
David Waters

Contents

Shade in each level of the circle as you feel more confident and ready for your exam.

How to use this book

This book uses a three-step approach to revision: **Knowledge**, **Retrieval**, and **Practice**. It is important that you do all three; they work together to make your revision effective.

Knowledge

Knowledge comes first. Each chapter starts with a **Knowledge Organiser**. These are clear easy-to-understand, concise summaries of the content that you need to know for your exam. The information is organised to show how one idea flows into the next so you can learn how everything is tied together, rather than lots of disconnected facts.

LINK

The **Link** box highlights a reference to a related topic you may want to refer to.

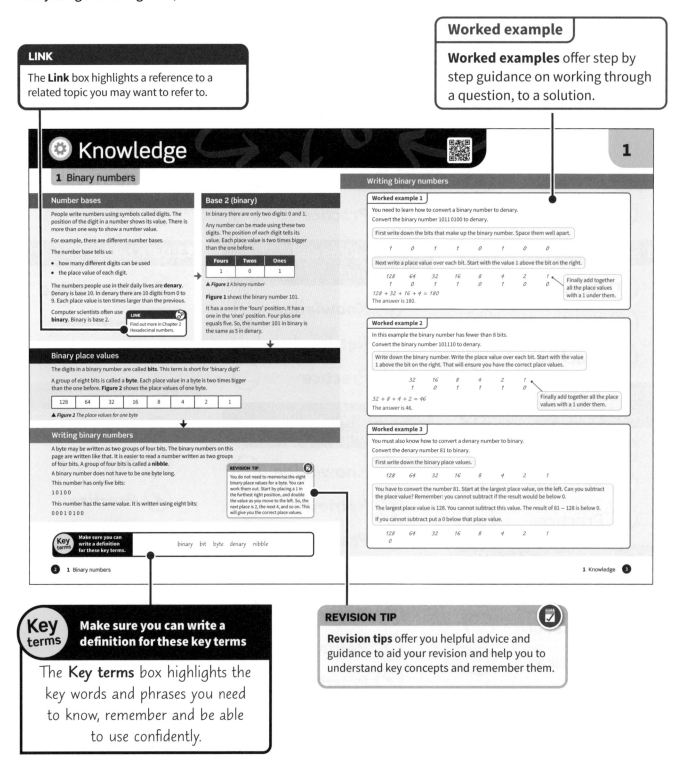

Worked example

Worked examples offer step by step guidance on working through a question, to a solution.

Knowledge

1

1 Binary numbers

Number bases

People write numbers using symbols called digits. The position of the digit in a number shows its value. There is more than one way to show a number value.

For example, there are different number bases.

The number base tells us:

- how many different digits can be used
- the place value of each digit.

The numbers people use in their daily lives are **denary**. Denary is base 10. In denary there are 10 digits from 0 to 9. Each place value is ten times larger than the previous.

Computer scientists often use **binary**. Binary is base 2.

LINK
Find out more in Chapter 2 Hexadecimal numbers.

Base 2 (binary)

In binary there are only two digits: 0 and 1.

Any number can be made using these two digits. The position of each digit tells its value. Each place value is two times bigger than the one before.

Fours	Twos	Ones
1	0	1

▲ *Figure 1 A binary number*

Figure 1 shows the binary number 101.

It has a one in the 'fours' position. It has a one in the 'ones' position. Four plus one equals five. So, the number 101 in binary is the same as 5 in denary.

Binary place values

The digits in a binary number are called **bits**. This term is short for 'binary digit'.

A group of eight bits is called a **byte**. Each place value in a byte is two times bigger than the one before. **Figure 2** shows the place values of one byte.

128	64	32	16	8	4	2	1

▲ *Figure 2 The place values for one byte*

Writing binary numbers

A byte may be written as two groups of four bits. The binary numbers on this page are written like that. It is easier to read a number written as two groups of four bits. A group of four bits is called a **nibble**.

A binary number does not have to be one byte long.

This number has only five bits:

10100

This number has the same value. It is written using eight bits:

0001 0100

REVISION TIP

You do not need to memorise the eight binary place values for a byte. You can work them out. Start by placing a 1 in the furthest right position, and double the value as you move to the left. So, the next place is 2, the next 4, and so on. This will give you the correct place values.

Key terms — Make sure you can write a definition for these key terms.

binary bit byte denary nibble

Writing binary numbers

Worked example 1

You need to learn how to convert a binary number to denary.

Convert the binary number 1011 0100 to denary.

First write down the bits that make up the binary number. Space them well apart.

1 0 1 1 0 1 0 0

Next write a place value over each bit. Start with the value 1 above the bit on the right.

128	64	32	16	8	4	2	1
1	0	1	1	0	1	0	0

Finally add together all the place values with a 1 under them.

128 + 32 + 16 + 4 = 180

The answer is 180.

Worked example 2

In this example the binary number has fewer than 8 bits.

Convert the binary number 101110 to denary.

Write down the binary number. Write the place value over each bit. Start with the value 1 above the bit on the right. That will ensure you have the correct place values.

32	16	8	4	2	1
1	0	1	1	1	0

Finally add together all the place values with a 1 under them.

32 + 8 + 4 + 2 = 46

The answer is 46.

Worked example 3

You must also know how to convert a denary number to binary.

Convert the denary number 81 to binary.

First write down the binary place values.

128 64 32 16 8 4 2 1

You have to convert the number 81. Start at the largest place value, on the left. Can you subtract the place value? Remember: you cannot subtract if the result would be below 0.

The largest place value is 128. You cannot subtract this value. The result of 81 – 128 is below 0.

If you cannot subtract put a 0 below that place value.

128	64	32	16	8	4	2	1
0							

2 1 Binary numbers

1 Knowledge 3

Key terms — Make sure you can write a definition for these key terms

The **Key terms** box highlights the key words and phrases you need to know, remember and be able to use confidently.

REVISION TIP

Revision tips offer you helpful advice and guidance to aid your revision and help you to understand key concepts and remember them.

The **Retrieval questions** help you learn and quickly recall the information you've acquired. These are short questions and answers about the content in the Knowledge Organiser you have just reviewed. Cover up the answers with some paper and write down as many answers as you can from memory. Check back to the Knowledge Organiser for any you got wrong, then cover the answers and attempt all the questions again until you can answer *all* the questions correctly.

Make sure you revisit the retrieval questions on different days to help them stick in your memory. You need to write down the answers each time, or say them out loud, otherwise it won't work.

Previous Questions

Each chapter also has some **Retrieval questions** from **previous chapters**. Answer these to see if you can remember the content from the earlier chapters. If you get the answers wrong, go back and do the Retrieval questions for the earlier chapters again.

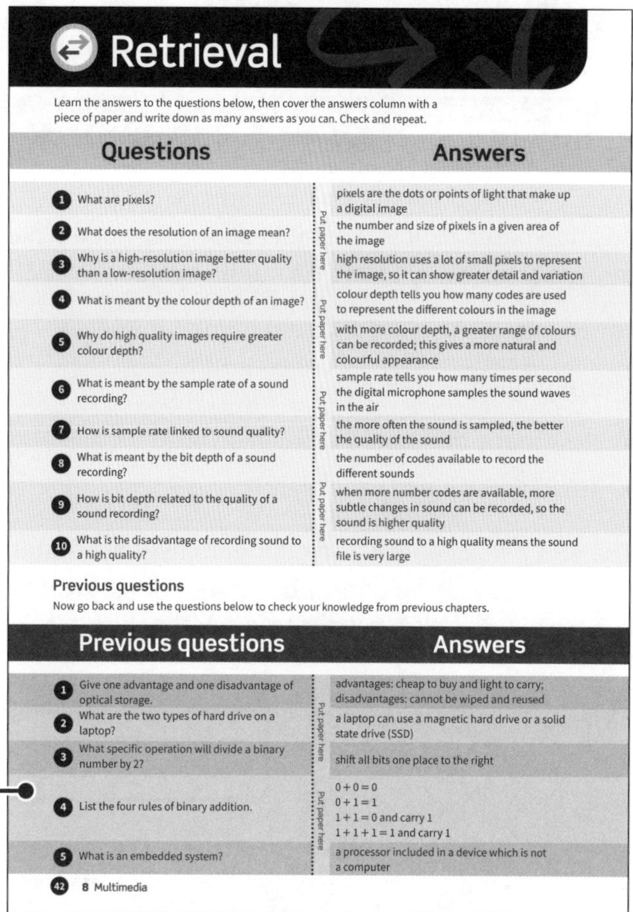

Retrieval

Learn the answers to the questions below, then cover the answers column with a piece of paper and write down as many answers as you can. Check and repeat.

	Questions	Answers
1	What are pixels?	pixels are the dots or points of light that make up a digital image
2	What does the resolution of an image mean?	the number and size of pixels in a given area of the image
3	Why is a high-resolution image better quality than a low-resolution image?	high resolution uses a lot of small pixels to represent the image, so it can show greater detail and variation
4	What is meant by the colour depth of an image?	colour depth tells you how many codes are used to represent the different colours in the image
5	Why do high quality images require greater colour depth?	with more colour depth, a greater range of colours can be recorded; this gives a more natural and colourful appearance
6	What is meant by the sample rate of a sound recording?	sample rate tells you how many times per second the digital microphone samples the sound waves in the air
7	How is sample rate linked to sound quality?	the more often the sound is sampled, the better the quality of the sound
8	What is meant by the bit depth of a sound recording?	the number of codes available to record the different sounds
9	How is bit depth related to the quality of a sound recording?	when more number codes are available, more subtle changes in sound can be recorded, so the sound is higher quality
10	What is the disadvantage of recording sound to a high quality?	recording sound to a high quality means the sound file is very large

Previous questions

Now go back and use the questions below to check your knowledge from previous chapters.

	Previous questions	Answers
1	Give one advantage and one disadvantage of optical storage.	advantages: cheap to buy and light to carry; disadvantages: cannot be wiped and reused
2	What are the two types of hard drive on a laptop?	a laptop can use a magnetic hard drive or a solid state drive (SSD)
3	What specific operation will divide a binary number by 2?	shift all bits one place to the right
4	List the four rules of binary addition.	0 + 0 = 0 0 + 1 = 1 1 + 1 = 0 and carry 1 1 + 1 + 1 = 1 and carry 1
5	What is an embedded system?	a processor included in a device which is not a computer

42 8 Multimedia

Once you think you know the Knowledge Organiser and Retrieval answers really well, you can move on to the final stage: **Practice**.

Each chapter has **exam-style questions**, including some questions from previous chapters, to help you apply all the knowledge you have learnt and can retrieve.

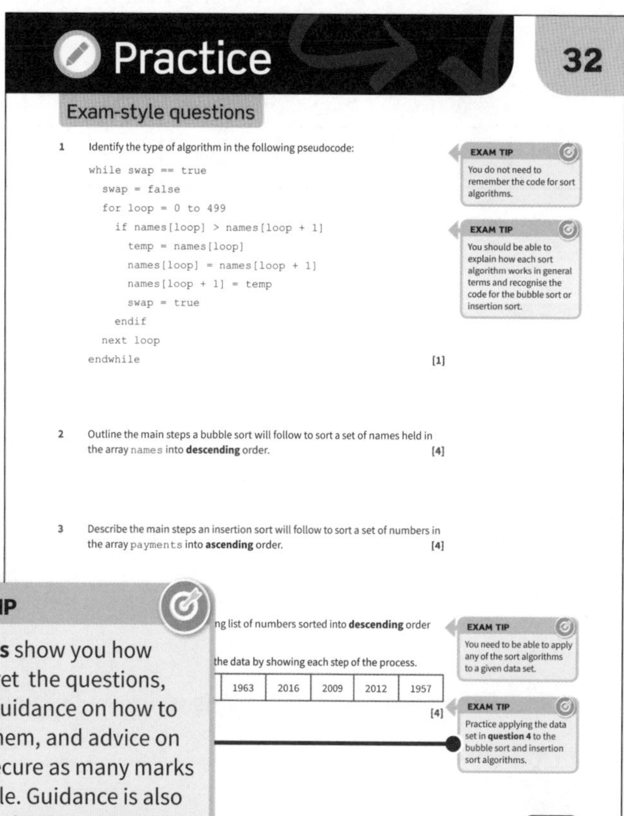

Practice 32

Exam-style questions

1 Identify the type of algorithm in the following pseudocode:

```
while swap == true
  swap = false
  for loop = 0 to 499
    if names[loop] > names[loop + 1]
      temp = names[loop]
      names[loop] = names[loop + 1]
      names[loop + 1] = temp
      swap = true
    endif
  next loop
endwhile
```

[1]

EXAM TIP: You do not need to remember the code for sort algorithms.

EXAM TIP: You should be able to explain how each sort algorithm works in general terms and recognise the code for the bubble sort or insertion sort.

2 Outline the main steps a bubble sort will follow to sort a set of names held in the array `names` into **descending** order. [4]

3 Describe the main steps an insertion sort will follow to sort a set of numbers in the array `payments` into **ascending** order. [4]

…ng list of numbers sorted into **descending** order

…the data by showing each step of the process.

1963	2016	2009	2012	1957

[4]

EXAM TIP: You need to be able to apply any of the sort algorithms to a given data set.

EXAM TIP: Practice applying the data set in **question 4** to the bubble sort and insertion sort algorithms.

32 Practice 177

EXAM TIP

Exam tips show you how to interpret the questions, provide guidance on how to answer them, and advice on how to secure as many marks as possible. Guidance is also offered on how to approach different command words.

Answers and Glossary

You can scan the QR code at any time to access the sample answers and mark schemes for all the exam-style questions, glossary containing definitions of the key terms, as well as further revision support go.oup.com/OR/GCSE/O/Comp

Knowledge

1 Binary numbers

Number bases

People write numbers using symbols called digits. The position of the digit in a number shows its value. There is more than one way to show a number value.

For example, there are different number bases.

The number base tells us:

- how many different digits can be used
- the place value of each digit.

The numbers people use in their daily lives are **denary**. Denary is base 10. In denary there are 10 digits from 0 to 9. Each place value is ten times larger than the previous.

Computer scientists often use **binary**. Binary is base 2.

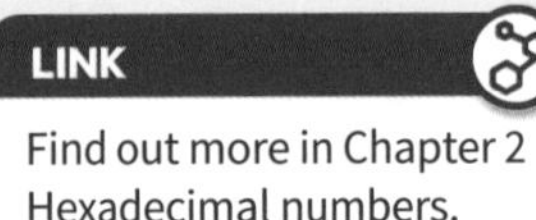
LINK
Find out more in Chapter 2 Hexadecimal numbers.

Base 2 (binary)

In binary there are only two digits: 0 and 1.

Any number can be made using these two digits. The position of each digit tells its value. Each place value is two times bigger than the one before.

Fours	Twos	Ones
1	0	1

▲ ***Figure 1*** *A binary number*

Figure 1 shows the binary number 101.

It has a one in the 'fours' position. It has a one in the 'ones' position. Four plus one equals five. So, the number 101 in binary is the same as 5 in denary.

Binary place values

The digits in a binary number are called **bits**. This term is short for 'binary digit'.

A group of eight bits is called a **byte**. Each place value in a byte is two times bigger than the one before. **Figure 2** shows the place values of one byte.

128	64	32	16	8	4	2	1

▲ ***Figure 2*** *The place values for one byte*

Writing binary numbers

A byte may be written as two groups of four bits. The binary numbers on this page are written like that. It is easier to read a number written as two groups of four bits. A group of four bits is called a **nibble**.

A binary number does not have to be one byte long.

This number has only five bits:

1 0100

This number has the same value. It is written using eight bits:

0001 0100

REVISION TIP

You do not need to memorise the eight binary place values for a byte. You can work them out. Start by placing a 1 in the furthest right position, and double the value as you move to the left. So, the next place is 2, the next 4, and so on. This will give you the correct place values.

Writing binary numbers

Worked example 1

You need to learn how to convert a binary number to denary.

Convert the binary number 1011 0100 to denary.

First write down the bits that make up the binary number. Space them well apart.

1	0	1	1	0	1	0	0

Next write a place value over each bit. Start with the value 1 above the bit on the right.

128	64	32	16	8	4	2	1
1	0	1	1	0	1	0	0

Finally add together all the place values with a 1 under them.

128 + 32 + 16 + 4 = 180

The answer is 180.

Worked example 2

In this example the binary number has fewer than 8 bits.

Convert the binary number 101110 to denary.

Write down the binary number. Write the place value over each bit. Start with the value 1 above the bit on the right. That will ensure you have the correct place values.

32	16	8	4	2	1
1	0	1	1	1	0

Finally add together all the place values with a 1 under them.

32 + 8 + 4 + 2 = 46

The answer is 46.

Worked example 3

You must also know how to convert a denary number to binary.

Convert the denary number 81 to binary.

First write down the binary place values.

128	64	32	16	8	4	2	1

You have to convert the number 81. Start at the largest place value, on the left. Can you subtract the place value? Remember: you cannot subtract if the result would be below 0.

The largest place value is 128. You cannot subtract this value. The result of 81 – 128 is below 0.

If you cannot subtract put a 0 below that place value.

128	64	32	16	8	4	2	1
0							

Knowledge

1 Binary numbers

Writing binary numbers

Worked example 3

The next place value is 64. You *can* subtract 64 from 81. 81 – 64 = 17.

If you can subtract put a 1 below that place value.

128	64	32	16	8	4	2	1
0	1						

The remaining denary value is 17. Look at the remaining place values. 17 is made of 16 and 1.

Put a 1 under the numbers 16 and 1, and a 0 in all the other places.

128	64	32	16	8	4	2	1
0	1	0	1	0	0	0	1

The answer is 0101 0001.

Worked example 4

Convert the denary number 214 to binary.

First write down the binary place values.

128 64 32 16 8 4 2 1

The largest place value is 128. You *can* subtract this value. 214 – 128 = 86.

Put a 1 below 128.

128	64	32	16	8	4	2	1
1							

The remaining denary value is 86. The next place heading is 64. 86 – 64 = 22.

Put a 1 below 64.

128	64	32	16	8	4	2	1
1	1						

The remaining denary value is 22. The next place heading is 32. You can't subtract 32 from this value.

Put a 0 below 32.

128	64	32	16	8	4	2	1
1	1	0					

Writing binary numbers

Worked example 4

The denary value is 22. The next place heading is 16. You can subtract 16. 22 – 16 = 6.

Put a 1 below 16.

128	64	32	16	8	4	2	1
1	1	0	1				

The remaining denary value is 6. Look at the remaining place values. 6 is made of 4 and 2.

Put a 1 below 4 and 2. Put a 0 below the other values.

Here is the final result.

128	64	32	16	8	4	2	1
1	1	0	1	0	1	1	0

The answer is 1101 0110.

REVISION TIP

Generate your own practice examples.

1. Think of a number between 0 and 255.
2. Convert it to binary.
3. Convert this back to denary.

You should end up with the number you started with. You can also do this activity with a study partner.

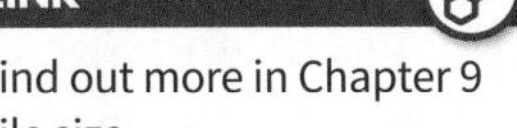

LINK

Find out more in Chapter 9 File size.

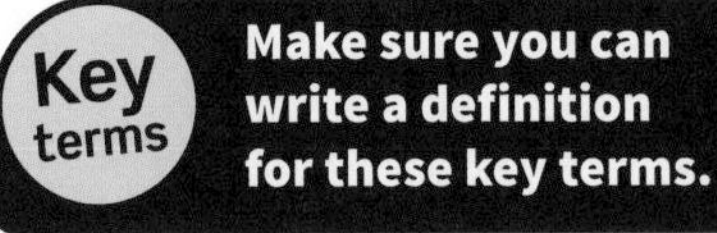
Key
terms
Make sure you can write a definition for these key terms.

binary bit byte denary nibble

Retrieval

Learn the answers to the questions below, then cover the answers column with a piece of paper and write down as many answers as you can. Check and repeat.

	Questions		Answers
1	What base is denary?	Put paper here	ten
2	What base is binary?		two
3	What digits can be used to make denary numbers?		0, 1, 2, 3, 4, 5, 6, 7, 8, 9
4	What digits can be used to make binary numbers?	Put paper here	1 and 0
5	What is the name for a single binary digit?		a bit
6	What is a byte?		a group of eight bits
7	What is a nibble?	Put paper here	a group of four bits
8	What are the binary place values of a byte?		128, 64, 32, 16, 8, 4, 2, 1
9	How do you convert a binary number to denary?		write the place values above the binary digits, then add together all the place values where there is a 1
10	How do you convert a denary number to binary?	Put paper here	subtract place values from the number, one at a time, starting with the largest value (128); do not subtract a value if the result would be a negative number; write a 1 under each place value that you can subtract, and a 0 under each place value that you cannot subtract; continue until you reach 0

Practice

Exam-style questions

1 Computers represent data in binary form.

Convert the denary number 127 into 8-bit binary. Show your working. **[2]**

> **EXAM TIP** 
>
> If a question asks you to 'show your working', always make sure you show how you have obtained your answer. Some of the marks are given specifically for your working.

> **EXAM TIP** 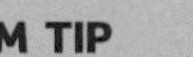 
>
> Start at the largest place value. Subtract the place values one by one. Write a 1 under every value that you can subtract. Remember: they can't go below 0.

2 Convert the binary number 1010 0111 into denary. Show your working. **[2]**

> **EXAM TIP** 
>
> One method is to write place values above the bits. Add together all the values with a 1 under them.

> **EXAM TIP** 
>
> If you can't remember the place values, start at the right with 1, and double the value each time you move to the left. That will give the values.

3 Identify the number of nibbles that make up one byte. **[1]**

> **EXAM TIP**
>
> Questions worth 1 mark are marked either right or wrong. You don't need to spend time showing your working.

Knowledge

2 Hexadecimal numbers

Hexadecimal is base 16

Hexadecimal is base 16. Hexadecimal has 16 digits.

The hexadecimal digits stand for the numbers 0 to 15.

Converting between **binary** and hexadecimal is easier than converting between binary and **denary**. People working with computers often use hexadecimal numbers for convenience.

REVISION TIP

You do not need to memorise the table of hexadecimal and binary values.

1. Write down the numbers from 0 to 15 in denary to make the first column.
2. Complete the hexadecimal column by copying the digits from 0 to 9, then switching to letters for the final six values.
3. Make the binary column by counting in binary from 0 to 1111.

You now have a complete conversion table that you can use to tackle any conversion question.

Letters are used for the digits above 9.

Hexadecimal	Binary	Denary
0	0000	0
1	0001	1
2	0010	2
3	0011	3
4	0100	4
5	0101	5
6	0110	6
7	0111	7
8	1000	8
9	1001	9
A	1010	10
B	1011	11
C	1100	12
D	1101	13
E	1110	14
F	1111	15

▲ ***Figure 1*** *Hexadecimal, binary and denary digits*

REVISION TIP

Generate your own practice examples.

1. Think of a number between 0 and 255.
2. Convert it to binary.
3. Convert the binary answer to hexadecimal.
4. Convert back to denary.

You should end up with the number you started with. You can also do this activity with a study partner.

LINK

Find out more in Chapter 1 Binary numbers.

REVISION TIP

For an extra challenge, vary the order of conversion. For example, first convert to hexadecimal, then to binary, then back to denary.

Hexadecimal place values

It is important to know the first two hexadecimal place values. The place values are 16 and 1.

Figure 2 shows the hexadecimal number 21.

Sixteens	Ones
2	1

▲ ***Figure 2*** *The hexadecimal number 21*

This hexadecimal number is two lots of 16 plus 1. $(2 \times 16) + 1 = 33$. So, the value is the same as 33 in denary.

Convert a hexadecimal number to denary

It is important to know the number values of the hexadecimal digits. To convert from hexadecimal to binary:

- multiply the value of the first digit by 16
- add the value of the second digit.

Worked example 1

This example question requires conversion from hexadecimal to denary.

Convert the hexadecimal number 2C to denary.

The first digit is 2. — Multiply the first digit by 16.

2 × 16 = 32

The second digit is C. The value of C is 12.

32 + 12 = 44 — Add the value of the second digit.

The answer is 44.

Worked example 2

Convert the hexadecimal number BF to denary.

The first digit is B. The value of B is 11.

11 × 16 = 176 — Multiply the first digit by 16.

The second digit is F. The value of F is 15.

176 + 15 = 191 — Add the value of the second digit.

The answer is 191.

Convert a denary number to hexadecimal

To convert a denary number to hexadecimal:

- divide the number by 16 and write the answer as a whole number, rounded down.
- calculate the remainder of this division and write that as the second digit.

Write both values using the hexadecimal system. If either value is greater than 9, use a hexadecimal digit.

Worked example 3

This example question requires conversion from denary to hexadecimal.

Convert the denary number 163 to hexadecimal.

163 divided by 16 is 10 remainder 3. — Divide the number by 16 using integer division.

The first digit is ten.

In hexadecimal this is A. — The integer part of the result is the first hexadecimal digit.

The remainder is 3. — The remainder is the second hexadecimal digit.

The answer is A3.

2 Hexadecimal numbers

Convert a denary number to hexadecimal

Worked example 4

Convert the denary number 45 to hexadecimal.

45 divided by 16 is 2 remainder 13. — Divide the number by 16 using integer division.

The first digit is 2. — The integer part of the result is the first hexadecimal digit.

The second digit is 13. — The remainder is the second hexadecimal digit.

13 is D in hexadecimal.

The answer is 2D.

Convert a binary number to hexadecimal

In the hexadecimal table, every group of four bits has a matching hexadecimal digit. If you know this table you can convert any binary number to hexadecimal.

- Split the bits into groups of four (nibbles).
- Write the matching hexadecimal digit under each nibble.

You do not need to convert the binary number to denary first.

REVISION TIP 

Knowing the hexadecimal table will make binary conversion easier.

Worked example 5

Convert the binary number 1111 0010 into hexadecimal.

1111 0011 — Write down the bits in groups of four.

1111 0011 — Write the matching hexadecimal digit under each group of four.

F 3

The answer is F3.

Worked example 6

Convert the binary number 0010 1010 into hexadecimal.

0010 1010 — Write down the bits in groups of four.

0010 1010 — Write the matching hexadecimal digit under each group of four.

2 A

The answer is 2A.

Convert a hexadecimal number to binary

To convert a hexadecimal number to binary, you do not need to convert the hexadecimal number to denary first.

- Write down the hexadecimal digits.
- Under each digit write the matching group of four bits.

Space the hexadecimal digits out well, so there is room to write four bits under each one.

Worked example 7

Convert the hexadecimal number B6 to binary

B 6 — Write the two hexadecimal digits.

B 6
1011 0110 — Write the matching four bits (nibble) under each digit.

The answer is 1011 0110.

Worked example 8

Convert the hexadecimal number 9E to binary.

9 E — Write the two hexadecimal digits.

9 E
1001 1110 — Write the matching four bits (nibble) under each.

The answer is 1001 1110.

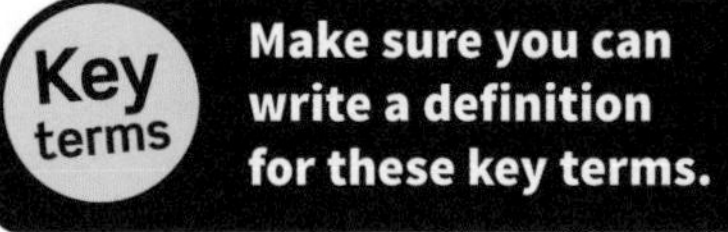
Key terms
Make sure you can write a definition for these key terms.

binary denary hexadecimal

Retrieval

Learn the answers to the questions below, then cover the answers column with a piece of paper and write down as many answers as you can. Check and repeat.

	Questions	Answers
1	What is hexadecimal?	hexadecimal is a base 16 number system
2	What denary values are represented by the hexadecimal digits?	0, 1, 2, 3, 4, 5, 6, 7, 8, 9, 10, 11, 12, 13, 14, 15
3	What are the hexadecimal digits?	0, 1, 2, 3, 4, 5, 6, 7, 8, 9, A, B, C, D, E, F
4	What are the place values of a two-digit hexadecimal number?	the place value of the first digit is 16; the place value of the second digit is 1
5	Explain the steps to convert a hexadecimal number to denary.	multiply the value of the first digit by 16 and add the value of the second digit
6	Explain the steps to convert a denary number to hexadecimal.	divide the number by 16; give the answer as a whole number plus remainder; the whole number is the first digit; the remainder is the second digit
7	Explain the steps to convert a binary number to hexadecimal.	break the binary number into nibbles (a group of four bits); write the equivalent hexadecimal digit under each nibble
8	Explain the steps to convert a hexadecimal number into binary.	write the hexadecimal digits; under each digit write the matching group of four bits

Put paper here

Put paper here

Put paper here

Previous questions

Now go back and use the questions below to check your knowledge from previous chapters.

	Previous questions	Answers
1	What is a nibble?	a group of four bits
2	What are the binary place values of a byte?	128, 64, 32, 16, 8, 4, 2, 1
3	How do you convert a binary number to denary?	write the place values above the binary digits, then add together all the place values where you see a 1
4	How do you convert a denary number to binary?	subtract place values from the number, one at a time, starting with the largest value (128); do not subtract a value if the result would be a negative number; write a 1 under each place value that you can subtract, and a 0 under each place value that you cannot subtract; continue until you reach 0
5	What digits can be used to make denary numbers?	0, 1, 2, 3, 4, 5, 6, 7, 8, 9
6	What digits can be used to make binary numbers?	1 and 0

Put paper here

Put paper here

Put paper here

Practice

Exam-style questions

1 Hexadecimal numbers are used as an alternative to binary or denary numbers.

Convert the hexadecimal number CB into denary. Show your working. **[2]**

EXAM TIP

Always be clear what number base you are using. Read the question carefully so you know what base to use.

2 Convert the denary number 210 into hexadecimal. Show your working. **[2]**

EXAM TIP

Knowing the hexadecimal table will make conversion easier.

EXAM TIP

Questions worth 2 marks often award 1 mark for the method and 1 mark for accuracy. Here you are asked to 'show your working'. This means a mark is available for the method you have used.

3 Convert the binary number 1010 0110 into hexadecimal. **[1]**

4 Convert the hexadecimal number C3 into binary. **[1]**

EXAM TIP

In the exam, you could write out the hexadecimal table on scrap paper to help you answer hexadecimal questions.

Knowledge

3 Binary arithmetic

Most significant bit

A byte is a group of eight bits. Each bit has a different place value.

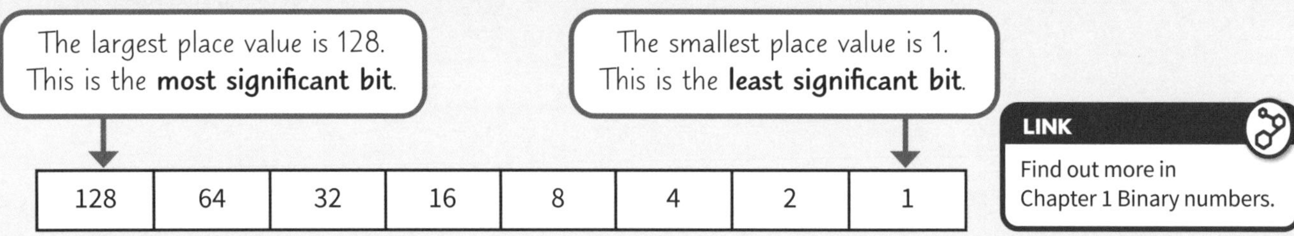
The largest place value is 128.
This is the **most significant bit**.
The smallest place value is 1.
This is the **least significant bit**.

128	64	32	16	8	4	2	1

▲ ***Figure 1*** *The place values in a byte*

LINK

Find out more in Chapter 1 Binary numbers.

Binary shift

Binary shift means moving all the bits in a number to the left or right. It is used to multiply or divide a binary number.

- Move the bits to the LEFT ← and the number gets two times bigger. The number is multiplied by two.
- Move the bits to the RIGHT → and the number gets two times smaller. The number is divided by two.

Shifting one place will multiply or divide by two.

Shifting two places will multiply or divide by four.

Figure 2 summarises how binary shift works.

Shifting bits left makes the number bigger.

Shifting bits right makes the number smaller.

	← Shift left	Shift right →
One place	Multiply by two	Divide by two
Two places	Multiply by four	Divide by four
Three places	Multiply by eight	Divide by eight

▲ ***Figure 2*** *Binary shift*

REVISION TIP

Right and left binary shift can be used to multiply and divide a binary number by a power of two. For example, by two, four or eight. You will not be asked to multiply or divide by any other numbers.

Worked example 1

It is important to know how to carry out a binary shift.

Complete a 1-place shift to the left on the binary number 0001 0100.
What operation have you carried out?

This number has bits in the 16 and 4 position. Shift both bits one place left.

- The 1 in position 16 shifts to position 32.
- The 1 in position 4 shifts to position 8.

Find the new position for each bit by counting to the left, or by looking at the number values.

Binary shift

Worked example 1

128	64	32	16	8	4	2	1
0	0	0	1	0	1	0	0

128	64	32	16	8	4	2	1
0	0	1	0	1	0	0	0

The new number is 0010 1000.

A binary shift to the left is a multiplication. A shift one place to the left multiplies by 2.

This is a multiplication by 2.

Check your answer by converting both values to denary. The second denary number should be twice as large as the first.

0001 0100 is 16 + 4 = 20 in denary.

0010 1000 is 32 + 8 = 40 in denary.

The second value is twice the value of the first so the answer is correct.

REVISION TIP

You are likely to be asked to perform simple shift operations (such as multiply by two) so make sure you know how to do this.

REVISION TIP

Remember the direction of shift:

- *left* to multiply (making the number larger)
- *right* to divide (making the number smaller).

To help you remember: place values to the left are larger, so shifting left makes the number larger.

Worked example 2

You must also know how to shift to the right.

Complete a 1-place shift to the right on the binary number 0001 0100. What operation have you carried out?

128	64	32	16	8	4	2	1
0	0	0	1	0	1	0	0

128	64	32	16	8	4	2	1
0	0	0	0	1	0	1	0

This number has bits in the 16 and 4 position. Shift both bits one place left.

- The 1 in position 16 shifts to position 8.
- The 1 in position 4 shifts to position 2.

Find the new position for each bit by counting to the left, or by looking at the number values.

The new number is 0000 1010.

This is a division by 2.

A binary shift to the right is a division. A shift one place to the right divides by two.

0001 0100 is 16 + 4 = 20 in denary.

0000 1010 is 8 + 2 = 10 in denary.

The second value is half the value of the first so the result is correct.

Check your answer by converting both values to denary. The second denary number should be twice as large as the first.

REVISION TIP 

Generate your own practice examples.

1. Write down a binary number.
2. Shift all the bits one place to the left.
3. Convert both numbers back to denary.

The second number should be exactly double the size of the first. You can also do this activity with a study partner. For variety, use a right shift to halve the size of a number.

Knowledge

3 Binary arithmetic

Binary addition

There are four rules of binary addition.

0 + 0 = 0

1 + 0 = 1

1 + 1 = 0 and carry 1

1 + 1 + 1 = 1 and carry 1

To add two binary numbers:

- write the numbers one above the other
- add up the bits in each column using the four rules of addition, starting from the right
- write the answer at the bottom of the column
- if there is a **carry bit**, write a 1 at the top of the next column to the left.

Worked example 3

It is important to know how to add two binary numbers.

What is the result of 0100 1011 + 0010 0011?

	0	1	0	0	1	0	1	1
+	0	0	1	0	0	0	1	1

Write the two numbers one above the other. Line up the place value columns.

Start on the right. Add up the numbers in the same column. Use the rules of binary addition.

							1	
	0	1	0	0	1	0	1	1
+	0	0	1	0	0	0	1	1
								0

The first column has two ones in it. The rule is '1 + 1 = 0 and carry 1'. Write 0 at the bottom of the column. Write the carry bit, 1, over the next column to the left.

						1	1	
	0	1	0	0	1	0	1	1
+	0	0	1	0	0	0	1	1
							1	0

The next column has three bits in it. The sum is 1 + 1 + 1. Write in the carry bit above the next column.

						1	1	
	0	1	0	0	1	0	1	1
+	0	0	1	0	0	0	1	1
	0	1	1	0	1	1	1	0

Complete the addition for each column in turn.

The answer is 0100 1011 + 0010 0011 = 0110 1110.

REVISION TIP

In any binary calculation you *must* show your working. When revising or practicing, include carry bits as an essential part of the activity.

REVISION TIP

Generate your own practice examples.

1. Write down two binary numbers.
2. Add the two numbers.
3. Convert all three numbers back to denary.

The first two numbers added together should give the final number. You can also do this activity with a study partner.

Overflow

You have seen that some calculations result in a carry bit. The carry bit is added to the next position along. Then the three bits in that column are added together. This gives the right result.

Sometimes there is a carry bit in the final position of the binary addition. In this case there is nowhere to put the carry bit. This is called an overflow error. An overflow error means the result of the addition will be wrong.

Overflow is caused when you try to store a number which is too big for the number of bits that are available. In a normal computer this can happen with very large numbers.

Worked example 4

You must be able to recognise an overflow error. This happens when there is a carry bit at the end of a binary addition. The result of the addition will be wrong.

What is the result of 1100 0000 + 1010 0000?

	1	1	0	0	0	0	0	0
+	1	0	1	0	0	0	0	0
	0	0	1	0	0	0	0	0

Write down the two numbers one above the other. Then add each column.

1 + 1 = 0 and carry 1

But there is nowhere to put the carry bit. The result of the addition is wrong. This is called an overflow error.

The left-most column contains this sum.

Key terms **Make sure you can write a definition for these key terms.**

binary shift carry bit least significant bit most significant bit

Retrieval

Learn the answers to the questions below, then cover the answers column with a piece of paper and write down as many answers as you can. Check and repeat.

	Questions	Answers
1	A byte has eight bits. What is the value of the most significant bit?	128
2	What is the value of the least significant bit in a byte?	1
3	What type of binary shift is used to multiply a binary number?	shift all bits to the left
4	What type of binary shift is used to divide a binary number?	shift all bits to the right
5	What specific operation will multiply a binary number by 4?	shift all bits two places to the left
6	What specific operation will divide a binary number by 2?	shift all bits one place to the right
7	List the four rules of binary addition.	$0 + 0 = 0$ $0 + 1 = 1$ $1 + 1 = 0$ and carry 1 $1 + 1 + 1 = 1$ and carry 1
8	Where do you write the carry bit in a binary addition?	at the top of the column to the left

Put paper here

Put paper here

Put paper here

Previous questions

Now go back and use the questions below to check your knowledge from previous chapters.

	Previous questions	Answers
1	What is the name for a single binary digit?	a bit
2	What is a byte?	a group of eight bits
3	What are the hexadecimal digits?	0, 1, 2, 3, 4, 5, 6, 7, 8, 9, A, B, C, D, E, F
4	What are the place values of a two-digit hexadecimal number?	the first place value is 16; the second place value is 1
5	Explain the steps to convert a hexadecimal number to denary?	the place value of the first digit is 16; the place value of the second digit is 1
6	Explain the steps to convert a denary number to hexadecimal.	divide the number by 16; give the answer as a whole number plus remainder; the whole number is the first digit; the remainder is the second digit

Put paper here

Put paper here

Practice

Exam-style questions

1 Computers carry out arithmetic on numbers in binary form.

Perform a binary shift of two places to the left on the 8-bit binary number 0011 0101. [1]

2 Describe the effect of a binary shift of three places to the right on a binary number. [2]

EXAM TIP

If the question asks you to 'describe' something you need to give a detailed account of a situation, event, pattern or process.

3 Add together the binary numbers 0111 0111 and 0010 0101. Show your working. [2]

EXAM TIP

If a binary addition question asks you to 'show your working', you should show the full column addition, including carry bits, as well as your final answer.

4 Explain what is meant by **overflow error** when doing binary addition. [3]

EXAM TIP

'Explain' questions require details. Make sure you explain what an overflow error is as well as how it applies to binary addition.

4 The processor

von Neumann architecture

Inside every computer is a processor. The processor is where all the work of the computer is carried out. The processor is joined to the other parts of a computer by electrical connections.

This is called **von Neumann architecture**.

All modern computers have the same basic structure, shown in **Figure 1**.

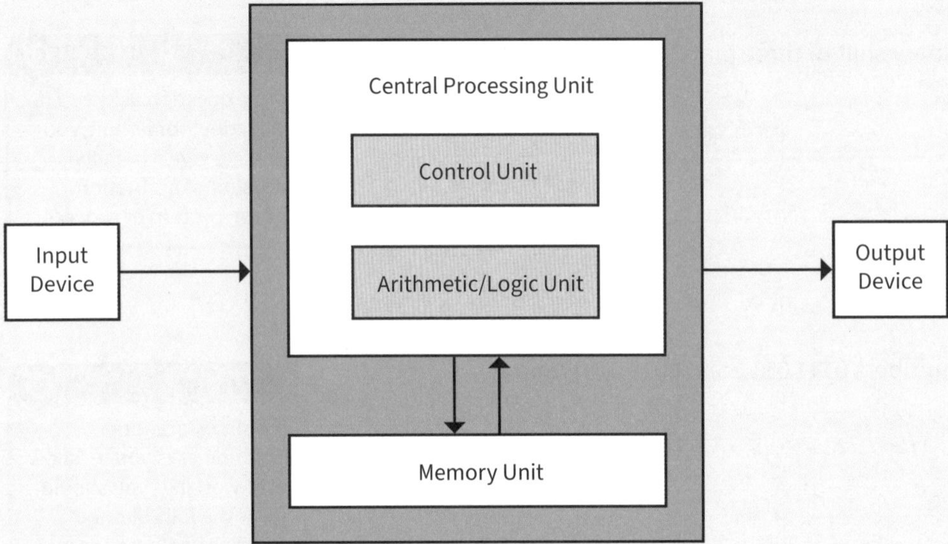

▲ ***Figure 1*** *von Neumann architecture*

The physical devices that make up a computer system are called hardware.

Input and output devices are connected to the processor These devices are called **peripherals**. The operating system controls the connection between the peripherals and the processor.

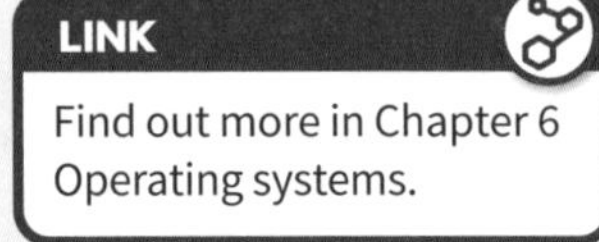

Find out more in Chapter 6 Operating systems.

Components of the processor

Inside the processor are three important components, shown in **Figure 2**.

Name	Also called	Role
The **control unit**	**CU**	Controls all the other parts of the computer. It sends out signals telling the other parts what to do.
The **arithmetic/ logic unit**	**ALU**	Processes data using binary maths and logic. It uses processes such as binary addition and binary shift.
The **memory unit**	**RAM** (random access memory)	Holds the data and instructions that the computer needs while it is working.

▲ ***Figure 2*** *Components of the processor*

The CU and ALU are sometimes grouped together and called the **CPU** (**central processing unit**).

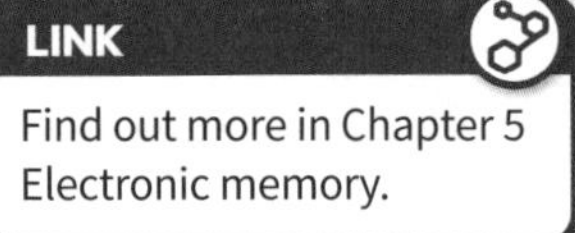

Find out more in Chapter 5 Electronic memory.

The fetch–execute cycle

Data and instructions are passed round the processor. This is called the **fetch–execute cycle**.

The fetch–execute cycle is carried out millions of times a second while the computer is running. It involves all parts of the processor.

The instructions that tell a computer what to do are called software.

REVISION TIP

'Execute' means to carry out an instruction.

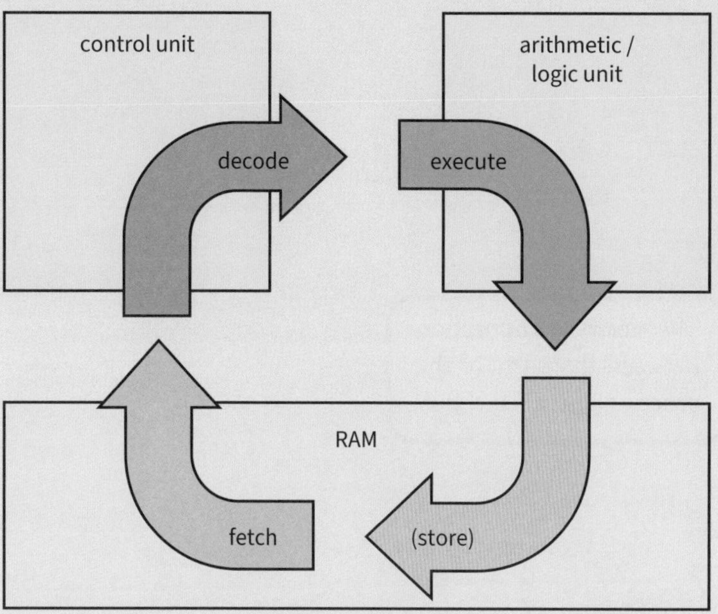

▲ ***Figure 3*** *The fetch–execute cycle*

REVISION TIP

Practise drawing the fetch–execute cycle diagram from memory. This is a helpful way to remember key facts in preparation for your exam.

The parts of the fetch–execute cycle are shown in **Figure 3**.

- Fetch: Instructions and data travel from RAM to the control unit. They are sent as binary numbers.
- Decode: The control unit changes a binary number from RAM into an instruction signal.
- Execute: The control unit sends the instruction signal to the ALU, which executes the instruction.
- Store: The result of the calculation is sent back to RAM to save for later.

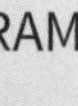

Clock signals

The control unit sends out regular pulses of electricity. These are called **clock signals**.

A modern computer has billions of pulses per second. The computer uses the clock signals to time the fetch–execute cycles. That means all the parts of the processor work together.

4 The processor

Multi-core computers

A computer processor carries out instructions one at a time. The CU and the ALU can only execute one instruction during each fetch–execute cycle.

However, many modern computers have several processors inside. That makes them work faster.

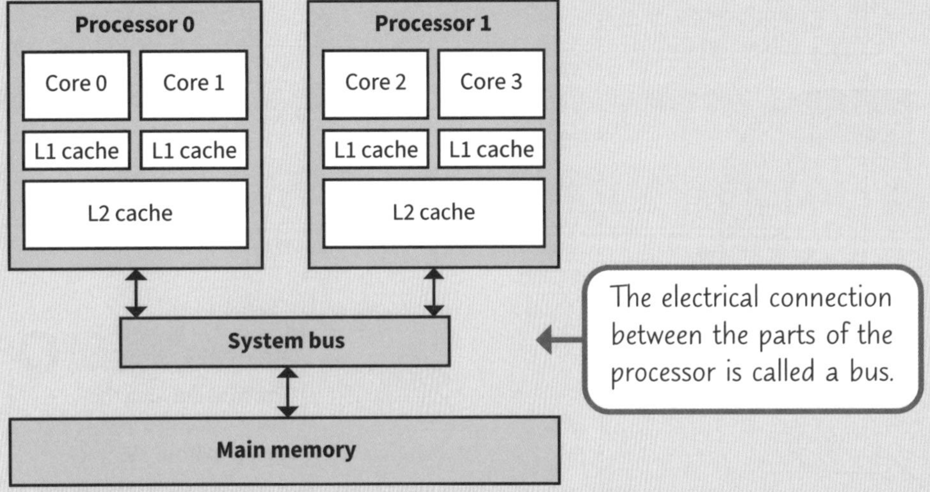

▲ ***Figure 4*** *Architecture of multicore processors*

- A dual-core processor has two CPUs and two ALUs. This type of processor can execute two instructions at the same time.
- A quad-core processor has four CPUs and four ALUs. This type of processor can execute four instructions at the same time.

▲ ***Figure 5*** *A dual core processor. Some modern computers even have an octo-core processor*

Cache memory

Most modern computers have an extra area of memory called a **cache**.

Cache memory is smaller than RAM. It cannot hold as much data or instructions. The cache memory is very close to the rest of the processor.

The CPU fetches data and instructions from cache memory at high speed. When the CPU fetches from cache memory, the fetch–execute cycle goes even faster.

Cache memory is used to store frequently used instructions and data.

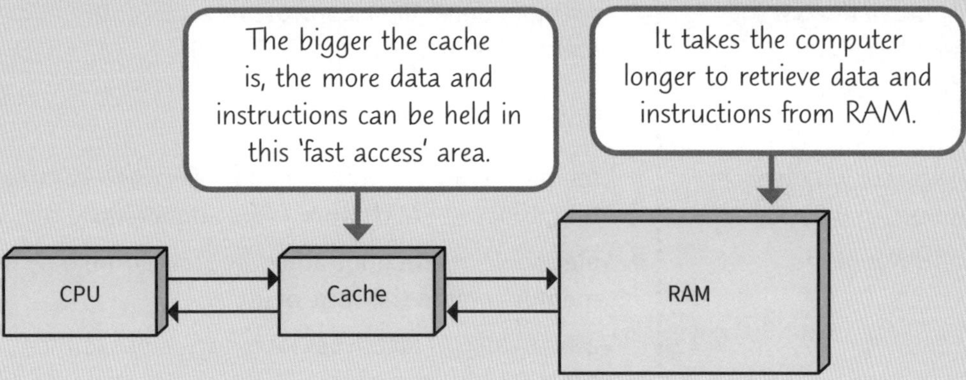

▲ ***Figure 6*** *Cache memory is the fastest memory in a computer*

Computer performance

Computer performance means how fast the computer goes.

A high-performance computer can process more instructions, more quickly. Some features of a computer processor are linked to faster processing.

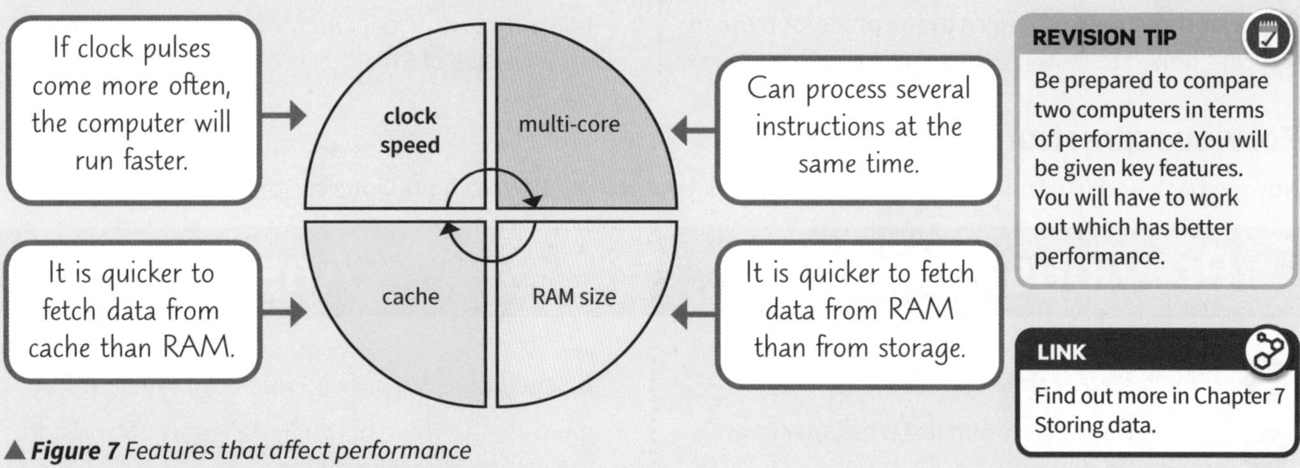

▲ ***Figure 7*** *Features that affect performance*

REVISION TIP

Be prepared to compare two computers in terms of performance. You will be given key features. You will have to work out which has better performance.

LINK

Find out more in Chapter 7 Storing data.

Key terms **Make sure you can write a definition for these key terms.**

arithmetic/logic unit (ALU) cache central processing unit (CPU) clock signals clock speed control unit (CU) fetch–execute cycle memory unit peripherals RAM von Neumann architecture

Retrieval

Learn the answers to the questions below, then cover the answers column with a piece of paper and write down as many answers as you can. Check and repeat.

	Questions	Answers
1	How does the control unit control the speed of the fetch–execute cycle?	the control unit sends clock signals to the rest of the processor
2	What is stored in the memory unit in the form of electronic numbers?	the memory unit stores instruction codes and data
3	State the full name and abbreviation for the three parts of the processor.	memory unit – RAM; control unit – CU; arithmetic/logic unit – ALU
4	What are the four stages of the fetch–execute cycle?	fetch, decode, execute, store
5	State the part(s) of the processor where each stage of the fetch–execute cycle takes place.	fetch – memory and control unit; decode – control unit; execute – ALU; store – ALU and memory
6	What happens at the fetch stage of the fetch–execute cycle?	electronic instructions and data travel from the memory unit to the control unit
7	What is cache memory?	a small area of fast-access memory, close to the processor
8	What is stored in cache memory?	it stores frequently used instructions and data
9	Explain how a computer could carry out more than one instruction during a single fetch–execute cycle.	if the processor has more than one core, more than one instruction can be carried out in the same fetch–execute cycle
10	How does increasing cache size increase processor speed?	it is quicker for the processor to fetch instructions and data from cache memory; if the cache memory is larger, then more of the instructions and data can be stored in this fast-access memory
11	List three more changes to the processor which are linked to faster processing speed.	increase clock speed; increase number of cores; increase size of RAM

Put paper here

Previous questions

Now go back and use the questions below to check your knowledge from previous chapters.

	Previous questions	Answers
1	What is hexadecimal?	hexadecimal is a base 16 number system
2	Explain the steps to convert a hexadecimal number to denary.	multiply the value of the first digit by 16 and add the value of the second digit
3	A byte has eight bits. What is the value of the most significant bit?	128
4	List the four rules of binary addition.	0 + 0 = 0 0 + 1 = 1 1 + 1 = 0 and carry 1 1 + 1 + 1 = 1 and carry 1

Put paper here

Practice

Exam-style questions

1 Modern computers use the basic structure known as the von Neumann architecture, which includes a processor. One component of the processor is the arithmetic/logic unit (ALU).

Explain the role of the ALU. **[3]**

EXAM TIP

'Explain' questions require a detailed account of how and why something happens.

2 Identify another component of the processor. **[1]**

3 Data and instructions are passed round the processor. This is called the fetch–execute cycle.

Complete the description of the fetch–execute cycle using the given list of terms.

Not all terms will be used.

ALU binary number cache command signal control unit decode signal decode denary number execute fetch hexadecimal number instruction signal processor RAM ROM

Fetch: Instructions and data travel from the .... to the ....

Decode: The control unit changes a .... from RAM into an instruction signal.

Execute: The control unit sends the .... to the ...., which executes the instruction.

The process repeats. **[5]**

4 Describe the effect of changing the processor in a computer from a dual-core processor to a quad-core processor. **[2]**

EXAM TIP

Practise drawing the components of the processor.

Knowledge

5 Electronic memory

Memory

The computer holds data and instructions using electricity. It holds data and instructions in RAM.

RAM is made of billions of **memory** locations. Each memory location has an address and some data. The address never changes. Just like a house address identifies a specific house, a memory address identifies a specific memory location.

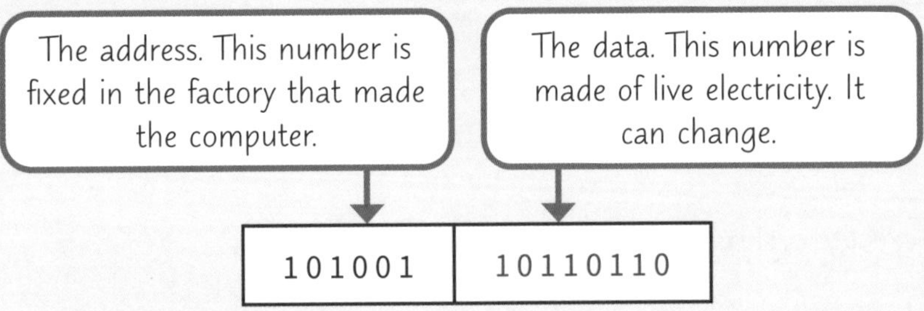

The address. This number is fixed in the factory that made the computer.
The data. This number is made of live electricity. It can change.
101001
10110110

▲ ***Figure 1*** *Memory location*

RAM is also called:

- memory unit
- electronic memory
- primary storage.

The data is held by live electrical circuits. This data can change whenever the electricity changes. It can change billions of times a second.

Memory that uses electricity to hold data is called **volatile** memory. RAM is volatile memory. Everything held in volatile memory is lost if the power is turned off.

Data and instructions are stored as electronic numbers in memory locations. They are digital.

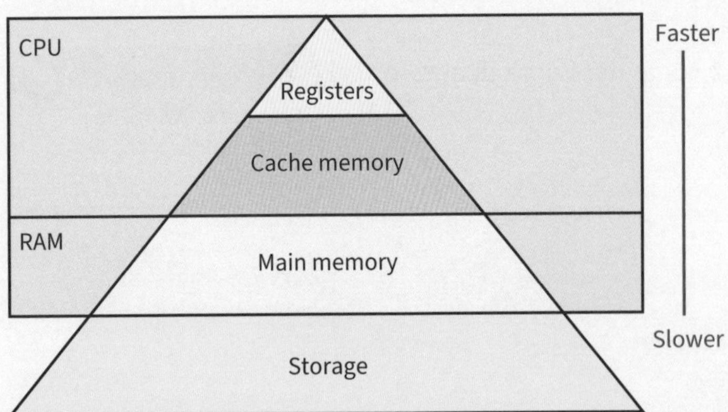

▲ ***Figure 2*** *Accessing CPU memory is faster than accessing RAM*

LINK

Find out more in Chapter 7 Storing data.

REVISION TIP

Digital means stored in number form.

RAM and ROM

Computers use another type of memory, read-only memory (**ROM**).
ROM cannot change.

The contents of ROM are fixed in the factory. ROM holds the start-up instructions for the computer. This is used when the power is turned on.

RAM	ROM
Volatile Can change High capacity Holds data and instructions	Is not volatile Read-only - cannot change Low capacity Holds start-up instructions

▲ ***Figure 3*** *Comparison of RAM and ROM*

Registers and the fetch-execute cycle

Instructions are fetched from RAM, and executed in the ALU.
This is the fetch–execute cycle.

Inside the processor are some tiny memory locations called **registers**.

A register has enough room for only one item. Some registers hold data. Some registers hold addresses.

LINK

Find out more in Chapter 4 The processor.

Name	Short name	What does it hold?	When is it used?	What is its job?
Program counter	**PC**	An address	The start of the cycle	The PC holds the address of the next line of the program. It counts through the program line by line.
Memory data register	**MDR**	Data	Fetch and store	During the fetch part of the cycle, the MDR holds the data that has been fetched from memory. During the store part of the cycle, it holds the data ready to be saved.
Memory address register	**MAR**	An address	Fetch and store	During the fetch part of the cycle, the MAR holds the memory address to fetch from. During the store part of the cycle, it holds the address to save to.
The accumulator	**ACC**	Data	Execute	Saves the results of each calculation carried out by the ALU.

▲ ***Figure 4*** *The registers*

REVISION TIP

The names of the registers will give you a clue about their jobs in the fetch–execute cycle. Accumulate means to 'collect together', and the accumulator collects and holds the results of calculations.

Knowledge

5 Electronic memory

Running software

When using a computer, you can use many different software applications. The computer loads and runs the software.

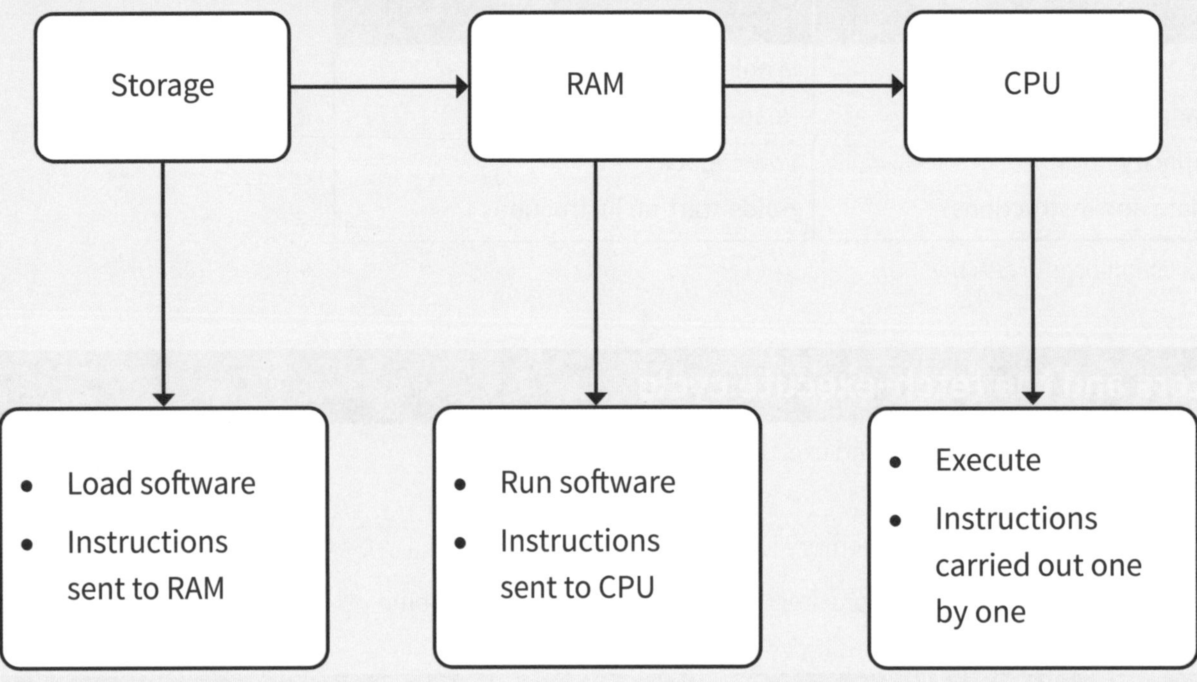

▲ ***Figure 5*** *Storage, RAM, and CPU*

Key terms **Make sure you can write a definition for these key terms.**

memory multi-tasking RAM registers (PC, MDR, MAR, ACC) ROM volatile

Multi-tasking

Most people use more than one application at the same time on the same computer. The name for this is **multi-tasking**. The computer multi-tasks by rapidly swapping between the different applications.

Each application has its own area of memory. The computer must keep track of the different areas of memory. It must 'fetch' instructions and data from each area in turn.

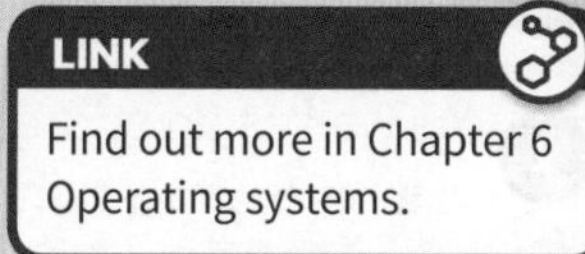

LINK

Find out more in Chapter 6 Operating systems.

The name for this is memory management. This is one of the tasks of the operating system.

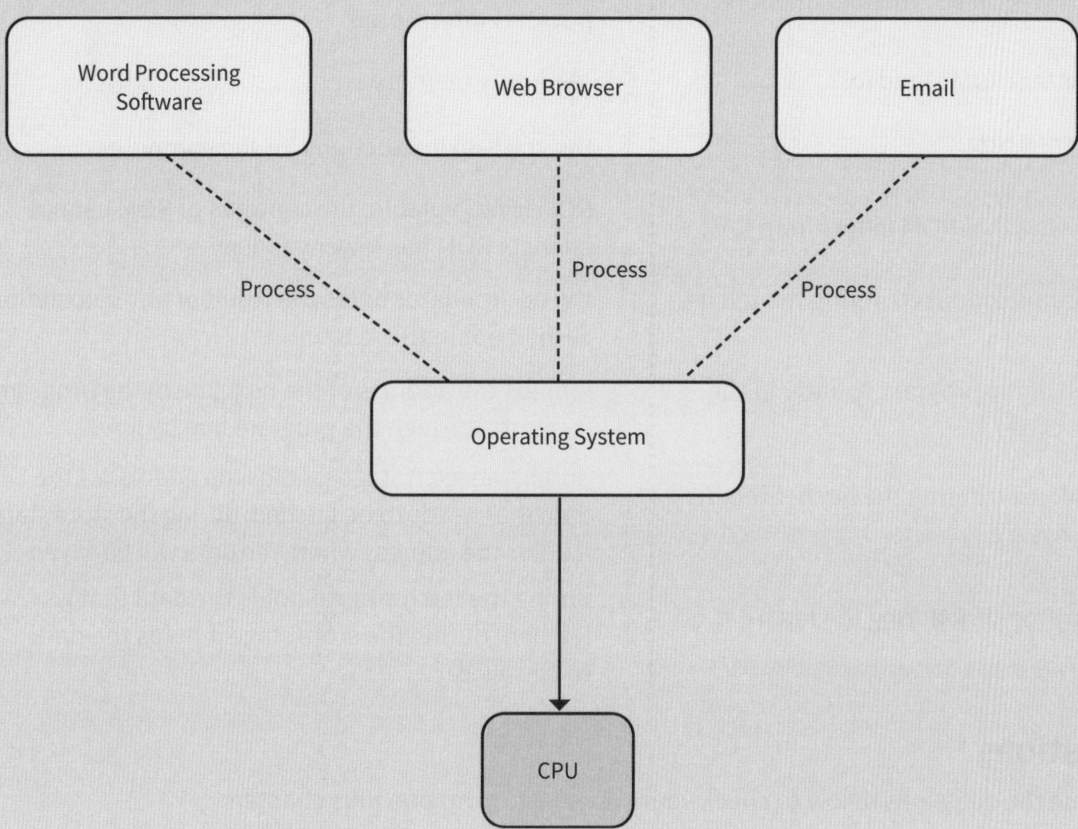

▲ ***Figure 6*** *Multi-tasking allows the user to perform more than one computer task at a time*

Retrieval

Learn the answers to the questions below, then cover the answers column with a piece of paper and write down as many answers as you can. Check and repeat.

	Questions	Answers
1	Every memory location in RAM has an address. What is an address?	a number that can be used to identify the location; it cannot change
2	As well as an address, what else can be found at a memory location?	the memory location holds data in electronic form; it can change
3	Explain why RAM is called 'volatile' memory.	because the content of the memory is lost if the power is interrupted
4	What do the letters ROM stand for?	read-only memory
5	What is stored in ROM?	the start-up instructions for the computer
6	List the main ways that ROM differs from RAM.	ROM is not volatile; the contents of ROM cannot change; ROM has lower capacity
7	How is the accumulator used during the fetch–execute cycle?	the accumulator holds the result of any calculation carried out in the ALU
8	What is the job of the program counter in the fetch–execute cycle?	it holds the address of the next line of the program; it counts through the program line by line
9	How is the MAR used during the fetch–execute cycle?	during the fetch stage it holds the address of the data that needs to be fetched; during the store stage it holds the address where the data will be saved
10	What is held by the MDR during the fetch–execute cycle?	during the fetch stage it holds the data that is fetched; during the store stage it holds the data to be saved

Put paper here

Previous questions

Now go back and use the questions below to check your knowledge from previous chapters.

	Previous questions	Answers
1	Explain the steps to convert a binary number to hexadecimal.	break the binary number into nibbles (a group of four bits); write the equivalent hexadecimal digit under each nibble
2	Explain the steps to convert a hexadecimal number into binary.	write the hexadecimal digits; under each digit write the matching group of four bits
3	What is cache memory? What is stored in cache memory?	a small area of fast-access memory, close to the processor; it stores frequently used instructions and data
4	What are the four stages of the fetch–execute cycle?	fetch, decode, execute, store
5	Explain how a computer could carry out more than one instruction during a single fetch–execute cycle.	if the processor has more than one core, more than one instruction can be carried out in the same fetch–execute cycle

Put paper here

Practice

Exam-style questions

1 A computer system uses RAM and ROM as its primary storage.

(a) Outline **one** difference between RAM and ROM. [1]

EXAM TIP

If a question asks for a difference, remember to give both perspectives.

(b) Identify **one** use for RAM and **one** use for ROM.

RAM

ROM [2]

2 Complete the table by writing the missing name or role of each of the given registers.

Register	Role
	To store intermediate logical or arithmetic data in multistep calculations.
Memory address register	
Memory data register	
Program counter	

[4]

Knowledge

6 Operating systems

Systems and applications software

Software means a set of instructions held in memory.

When the computer runs software, it carries out the instructions.

There are two types of software, shown in **Figure 1**.

Applications software	Systems software
Software to help the human user. This includes programming software, social media apps, and games.	Software that manages and organises the computer. This includes the operating system, device drivers, and utilities.

▲ ***Figure 1*** *Types of software*

REVISION TIP 

Think about what applications and systems software you use, to help give context to your answers and build your understanding.

Operating systems

An **operating system** bundles together all the systems software needed to make the computer work properly. When you buy a computer, the operating system is usually already installed.

Functions of an operating system	What this function means
User interface	Controls how you interact with the computer. How you give instructions and see results.
Memory management	Controls how data and instructions are stored in RAM. This is more difficult if there is multi-tasking because many different tasks are using space in memory to hold instructions and data. The operating system must make sure the different tasks do not affect each other.
Peripheral management	Controls the flow of data between the processor and the peripherals.
File management	Organises files in secondary storage. Lets you open, copy, or delete files.
User management	Keeps track of multiple users, so each one sees their own work files. Users may have IDs and passwords.

▲ ***Figure 2*** *Parts of an operating system*

LINK 

Find out more in Chapter 4 The processor, Chapter 7 Storing data and Chapter 12 Online security.

Make sure you can write a definition for these key terms.

device driver embedded system operating system user interface utilities

Device drivers

You can connect many different devices to a computer. For example, a mouse, a keyboard, or a game pad. The connection can be through a wire or wireless.

The software that lets your computer control the peripheral is called a **device driver**. The operating system usually includes all the device drivers you need when you get it. Sometimes you need to download a new driver when you buy a new device.

▶ ***Figure 3*** *If you buy a non-standard device you may need to download a device driver*

Utilities

System software can do many useful tasks. Most are provided as part of an operating system. However, you can buy or download other types of system software if you need them. These are called **utilities**. Utility software typically does one job.

Task of a utility	Meaning	Find out more in chapter
Defragmentation	Tidying up secondary storage, so that files are stored in continuous blocks.	7: Storing data
Encryption	Protecting messages using a secret code system.	12: Online security
Compression	Making file sizes smaller to use less storage.	9: File size

▲ ***Figure 4*** *Some operating system utilities*

Embedded systems

Digital devices include tablets, phones, and laptops. All digital devices have a processor in them. But sometimes other sorts of devices have a processor in them. A processor inside a device like this is called an **embedded system**.

Devices such as cars, fridges, air-conditioning systems and heart pacemakers can all have embedded systems.

The processor embedded in the device helps it to do simple tasks, such as maintain the temperature of a fridge, or check the fuel used by a car. It can let you exchange signals between your phone and the device.

▲ ***Figure 5*** *Embedded processors control electrical and mechanical functions*

- An embedded operating system supports a few tasks, relevant to the device.
- The device has a simple user interface, limited to those tasks.
- The functions of the device are unlikely to change.

The user interface

One of the jobs of the operating system is to provide a **user interface**.

The user interface is how you control the computer. You can use the keyboard, mouse or touchscreen to tell the computer what to do. Or you can speak voice commands.

The computer might use sounds, text, images, or vibrations to send information and signals to you. Look out for examples of user interfaces in the devices you use.

REVISION TIP

What examples of user interfaces can you find in the devices you use? Think about how you interact with these devices.

▶ ***Figure 6*** *A graphical user interface is common in most PCs and laptops.*

Retrieval

Learn the answers to the questions below, then cover the answers column with a piece of paper and write down as many answers as you can. Check and repeat.

	Questions	Answers
1	What is an operating system?	the bundle of systems software, which is already installed on your computer when you buy it
2	Give three examples of utility software.	defragmentation, compression, encryption
3	Define a user interface.	the user interface allows the user to work with the computer sending and receiving information
4	List four ways the user can control the computer.	keyboard, mouse, touchscreen, voice command
5	List four ways that a computer can send information or signals to the user.	sounds, text, images, vibrations
6	What is an embedded system?	a processor included in a device which is not a computer
7	What tasks are involved in file management?	organising files in secondary storage; lets the user open, copy, move or delete files
8	What is a peripheral device?	a peripheral device is a device attached to the computer processor
9	Give two typical functions of peripheral devices.	for example, input and output devices
10	What is the purpose of user management?	user management is needed if there are many users of the system; the operating system keeps track of multiple users, so each one sees their own work files
11	Explain why memory management is more difficult if the computer is multi-tasking.	memory management means keeping track of the area of memory where instructions and data are held; when the computer is multi-tasking more than one area of memory is in use at the same time

Put paper here

Previous questions

Now go back and use the questions below to check your knowledge from previous chapters.

	Previous questions	Answers
1	Every memory location in RAM has an address. What is an address?	a number that can be used to identify the location; it cannot change
2	As well as an address, what else can be found at a memory location?	the memory location holds data in electronic form; it can change
3	How does the control unit control the speed of the fetch–execute cycle?	the control unit sends clock signals to the rest of the processor
4	State the full name and abbreviation for the three parts of the processor.	memory unit – RAM; control unit – CU; arithmetic/logic unit – ALU

Put paper here

Exam-style questions

1 File management is a function of an operating system.

Identify **three** features of file management **[3]**

2 A computer system has been supplied with utility software.

Identify **two** types of utility software **and** describe the purpose of each type.

Utility software 1

Purpose

Utility software 2

Purpose **[6]**

EXAM TIP

Exam questions may refer to **purpose** or **function**. For an operating system, an example of **purpose** is to manage and control the computer. Examples of **functions** are user interface or memory management. Read the question carefully so you know which answer to give.

3 A washing machine is a device that could be controlled by an embedded system.

Outline the main characteristics of an embedded system. **[3]**

EXAM TIP 

If a question doesn't ask for a specific number of points, look at the number of marks to be awarded. Make sure you include as many distinct points in your answer as there are marks available.

Knowledge

7 Storing data

Digital data

The processor fetches data and instructions during the fetch-execute cycle.

The processor can only process **digital data**. Digital data is made of on/off signals that can be represented using binary numbers.

Digital data is held in files. A file is a collection of data or instructions. You may be able to read the file, or write to the file. Files have names. You can rename, delete or copy files.

LINK

Find out more in Chapter 12 Online security.

REVISION TIP

As you work through each section, think about how you use the technology. Make notes on the page to help you link the theory to your practical understanding.

RAM (Digital Memory)

Data file

- Holds text, image, sound, video
  - Read the file – look at the text, listen to the sound, etc.
  - Write to the file – change the content of the file

Software file

- Holds instructions
  - Run the file – carry out the instructions

Memory and storage

As well as memory, a computer needs storage. That is because memory is volatile. **Figure 1** shows the features of memory and storage.

Memory	Storage
Sometimes called **primary storage**.	Sometimes called **secondary storage**.
• holds digital data and instructions • uses on/off electrical signals • needs electricity to work • if the electricity is turned off the contents of memory are lost • faster access	• holds digital data and instructions • uses a method of storage that does not need electricity • keeps a copy of data and instructions when they are not in use • slower access

▲ ***Figure 1*** *Features of memory and storage*

Both memory and storage are needed by the computer.

- **Memory**: The processor can fetch digital data quickly from memory.
- **Storage**: Keeps digital data so it is not lost when the computer is turned off.

You should always copy your files to storage before you turn the computer off.

LINK

Find out more in Chapter 5 Electronic memory.

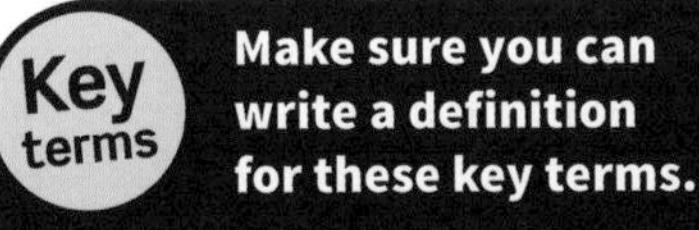

Key terms **Make sure you can write a definition for these key terms.**

digital data flash storage magnetic storage memory optical storage primary storage secondary storage solid state storage storage virtual memory

Virtual memory

Multi-tasking means many different files are opened in memory.

If you open too many files, your computer can run out of space in RAM. When this happens the computer has to use storage instead of memory. The files the computer needs are sent to storage. The computer must fetch them from storage instead of from RAM.

When storage is used as memory, it is called **virtual memory**. Access to virtual memory is slow. So if the computer uses virtual memory, it will go more slowly.

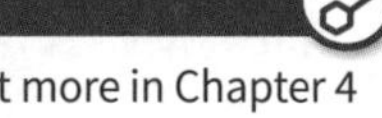

LINK

Find out more in Chapter 4 The processor.

Types of storage

There are three important ways to store files without electricity:

- **optical**, e.g. CD, DVD, BluRay
- **magnetic**, e.g. hard drive of a computer, magnetic tape
- **flash** (also called **solid state**), e.g. USB stick, solid-state drive, SD card.

REVISION TIP

Note down differences between each type of storage device/medium.

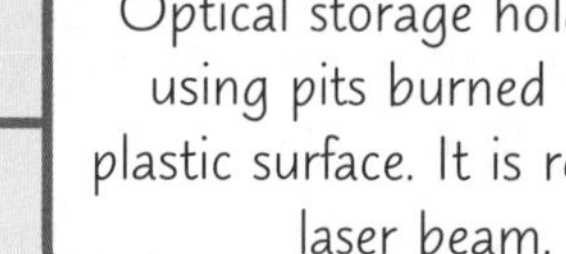

Optical storage holds data using pits burned into a plastic surface. It is read by a laser beam.

Magnetic storage holds data using grains of magnetised metal.

Flash memory holds data using electrons trapped in solid matter. It is also called solid state storage.

▲ ***Figure 2*** *The three main types of storage*

Storage features

Each type of storage has benefits and limitations, as shown in **Figure 3**.

Type of storage	Benefits	Limitations	Typical uses
Optical	cheap to buy, light to carry	cannot be wiped and reused (usually)	distributing music, games, and videos
Magnetic	holds a lot of data	takes up space, heavy to carry, can be broken if dropped	hard disk of a desktop computer
Flash	small, light, and high capacity	more expensive than the alternatives	personal storage, mobile devices

▲ ***Figure 3*** *Benefits and limitations of different storage methods*

REVISION TIP

Compare the advantages and disadvantages for each storage device.

Choose the right storage

When choosing storage you need to think about:

- storage needs: for example, lightweight storage, cheap storage
- storage features: match the benefits and limitations to your storage needs.

Cloud storage

Cloud storage means storage that you access through an internet connection.

The storage is held remotely on a large computer owned by a company such as Google or Microsoft. Cloud storage does not refer to the way the data is stored. It tells you that the storage is far away from your computer.

Retrieval

Learn the answers to the questions below, then cover the answers column with a piece of paper and write down as many answers as you can. Check and repeat.

Questions	Answers
1 Give other names for primary storage.	memory, RAM
2 Describe what virtual memory means.	when the computer runs out of space in memory, it moves some of the instructions and data from memory to storage
3 Explain why using virtual memory makes the computer go more slowly.	it takes longer for the computer to fetch data and instructions from storage that it does from RAM
4 Explain what happens to the data and instructions in storage when the electricity is turned off.	data and instructions are held in storage without being lost if the electricity is turned off
5 Give three types of optical storage.	CD, DVD, BluRay
6 Give one advantage and one disadvantage of optical storage.	advantages: cheap to buy and light to carry; disadvantages: cannot be wiped and reused
7 What are the two types of hard drive on a laptop?	a laptop can use a magnetic hard drive or a solid state drive (SSD)
8 What are the disadvantages of the two types of hard drive?	magnetic hard drives are heavier and easier to break; an SSD is more expensive
9 What are the advantages of the two types of hard drive?	magnetic hard drives are cheaper; an SSD holds more data and is lighter and stronger
10 How does a flash memory stick hold data?	flash memory uses electrons trapped within solid matter to store data
11 What is the main disadvantage of using flash memory?	it is more expensive than other types of memory

Put paper here

Previous questions

Now go back and use the questions below to check your knowledge from previous chapters.

Previous questions	Answers
1 What is an operating system?	the bundle of systems software, which is already installed on your computer when you buy it
2 Give three examples of utility software.	defragmentation, compression, encryption
3 List the main ways that ROM differs from RAM.	ROM is not volatile; the contents of ROM cannot change; ROM has lower capacity
4 How is the accumulator used during the fetch–execute cycle?	the accumulator holds the result of any calculation carried out in the ALU

Put paper here

Exam-style questions

1 Computers need both primary and secondary storage.

Outline **one** reason why a computer needs secondary storage. **[2]**

> **EXAM TIP**
>
> Some questions will ask about types of **storage**, others will ask about types of **storage devices**. Read the question carefully to make sure you don't mix them up.

2 One common type of storage is optical.

Identify **two** more types of storage. **[2]**

3 Give **two** advantages and **two** disadvantages of a solid state drive compared with a hard disk drive. **[4]**

> **EXAM TIP**
>
> Be specific in your answers and avoid general statements.

4 Explain why virtual memory may be needed in a computer system. **[3]**

> **EXAM TIP**
>
> If an 'explain' question asks you to 'explain why' it is looking for the reasons why something is needed, not how it works.

Knowledge

8 Multimedia

Digital images

Multimedia means digital recording of sounds and images.

Images are stored inside the computer as a grid of **pixels**. Pixel is another way of saying 'picture element'.

The colour of each pixel is saved as a colour code number. A grid of coloured dots is saved as a file of many number codes.

◀ *Figure 1 Digital images are made of a grid of dots or points of light called pixels.*

LINK

Find out more in Chapter 7 Storing data.

Image quality

Two factors affect the quality of an image. They are **resolution** and **colour depth**.

	Resolution	Colour depth	What is the effect?
High quality image	High resolution: the image is made of lots of small pixels to give a sharp and detailed image	Increased colour depth: lots of different colour codes	An image with lots of realistic colours and sharp details
Low quality image	Low resolution: the image is made of fewer, larger pixels. The image is blurry or lacks detail	Reduced colour depth: fewer colour codes, or just black and white	A blurry image, or an image with few details, using only a few simple colours

▲ *Figure 2 The effects of resolution and colour depth*

A high-quality image has more pixels and each pixel is stored using more bytes. The quality is higher but the file is larger.

A low-resolution image can be blurry. The pixels are larger so there is less detail.

▲ *Figure 3 A low resolution image compared with a high resolution image.*

▲ *Figure 4 Increasing colour depth, as shown here, allows more realistic colours.*

Digital video, such as a movie, uses both sound and images. Video can be stored in high quality if the sounds and images are high quality. Digital video files can be very large.

REVISION TIP

A high quality image has high resolution and high colour depth. This makes the image more realistic but increases the file size.

REVISION TIP

Metadata stores additional image information, such as height.

Key terms Make sure you can write a definition for these key terms.

bit depth   colour depth   pixel   resolution   sample rate

Digital sound

Sounds are also held as number data.

Sound waves travel through the air. Changes in the wave pattern make different sounds. High frequency sounds are higher in pitch. High amplitude sounds are louder. The sound waves are picked up by a digital microphone and turned into number codes.

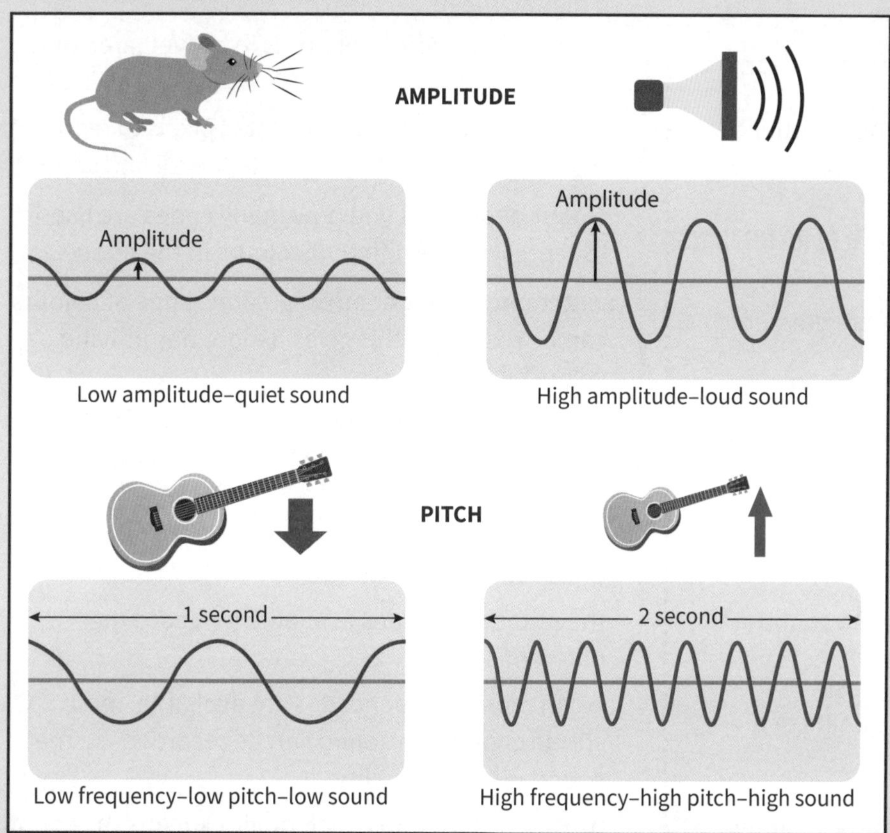

◀ ***Figure 5*** *Sound travels through the air as waves.*

Sound quality

Two factors affect the quality of a sound recording: **sample rate** and **bit depth**.

	Sample rate	Bit depth	What is the effect?
High quality sound	High sample rate: the sound is sampled more than a hundred thousand times per second by the microphone	Increased bit depth: lots of different sound codes are used	When it is played back the sound is realistic and natural – like real life
Low quality sound	Low sample rate: the sound is sampled less often, so some subtle variations might be missed	Reduced bit depth: fewer sound codes are used, so the sound is simplified	The sound is distorted or less realistic

▲ ***Figure 6*** *The effects of sample rate and bit depth*

The sample rate is measured in hertz (Hz). Hertz means 'how many per second'. So 44 000 Hz means 44 000 samples per second.

A high-quality sound file has more samples in it and each sample uses more bits. The quality is higher but the file is larger.

LINK

Find out more in Chapter 9 File size.

Retrieval

Learn the answers to the questions below, then cover the answers column with a piece of paper and write down as many answers as you can. Check and repeat.

Questions	Answers
1 What are pixels?	pixels are the dots or points of light that make up a digital image
2 What does the resolution of an image mean?	the number and size of pixels in a given area of the image
3 Why is a high-resolution image better quality than a low-resolution image?	high resolution uses a lot of small pixels to represent the image, so it can show greater detail and variation
4 What is meant by the colour depth of an image?	colour depth tells you how many codes are used to represent the different colours in the image
5 Why do high quality images require greater colour depth?	with more colour depth, a greater range of colours can be recorded; this gives a more natural and colourful appearance
6 What is meant by the sample rate of a sound recording?	sample rate tells you how many times per second the digital microphone samples the sound waves in the air
7 How is sample rate linked to sound quality?	the more often the sound is sampled, the better the quality of the sound
8 What is meant by the bit depth of a sound recording?	the number of codes available to record the different sounds
9 How is bit depth related to the quality of a sound recording?	when more number codes are available, more subtle changes in sound can be recorded, so the sound is higher quality
10 What is the disadvantage of recording sound to a high quality?	recording sound to a high quality means the sound file is very large

Put paper here

Previous questions

Now go back and use the questions below to check your knowledge from previous chapters.

Previous questions	Answers
1 Give one advantage and one disadvantage of optical storage.	advantages: cheap to buy and light to carry; disadvantages: cannot be wiped and reused
2 What are the two types of hard drive on a laptop?	a laptop can use a magnetic hard drive or a solid state drive (SSD)
3 What specific operation will divide a binary number by 2?	shift all bits one place to the right
4 List the four rules of binary addition.	0 + 0 = 0 0 + 1 = 1 1 + 1 = 0 and carry 1 1 + 1 + 1 = 1 and carry 1
5 What is an embedded system?	a processor included in a device which is not a computer

Put paper here

Exam-style questions

1 A pixel representing a shade of blue is given by the binary number 0110 0011.

Identify the hexadecimal number that represents the given binary number. **[1]**

2 Explain how changing the resolution can affect the size of an image file. **[3]**

EXAM TIP

Underline keywords in the question. Check you have included or linked to these in your final answer.

3 A music track has been recorded and stored as a sound file.

Tick (✓) **one or more** boxes on each row to identify the effect(s) that each change will have on the sound file.

Change	Sound quality increases	Sound quality decreases	File size increases	File size decreases
Sample rate changes from 96 000 hertz to 48 000 hertz				
Bit depth changes from 16 bits to 24 bits				

[2]

EXAM TIP

Some questions require multiple boxes to be ticked in tables. Other questions will need only one tick per row. Read the question carefully to make sure you tick the correct number of boxes.

4 A music concert is recorded on a mobile phone.

Describe **one** reason why the sound cannot be stored directly to the mobile phone without first being converted. **[2]**

EXAM TIP

Additional answer pages will be provided in your exam if you need them. Don't try to squeeze everything into the spaces provided.

9 File size

Numbers and file size

You have learned to represent number values in binary. It takes more bits to store larger numbers.

How much storage	How many bits	Number range
1 nibble	4	0 to 15
1 byte	8	0 to 255
2 bytes	16	0 to 65 536
4 bytes	32	More than 4 billion

▲ ***Figure 1*** *The number ranges that can be stored in different file sizes*

LINK

Find out more in Chapter 1 Binary numbers.

To store a wider range of numbers you need more storage space for each number.

Digital text

Characters are the letters and other symbols you can type on a keyboard. Text data is made of characters. Text can be held in digital form. To do this, each character is given a code number.

The name for the set of characters and their code numbers is a character set.

Two common character sets are **ASCII** and **Unicode**.

ASCII	
Character	**Code number**
A	65
B	66
C	67
D	68

▲ ***Figure 2*** *ASCII character set*

▲ ***Figure 3*** *Unicode has many more characters than ASCII, including emojis*

REVISION TIP 

Remember! Character sets are logically ordered. For example, the code for 'D' will be one higher than the code for 'C'.

ASCII	Unicode
• fewer than 255 codes • each code takes 1 byte • only includes basic keyboard characters	• many thousands of codes • each code takes between 1 and 4 bytes • has all global alphabets, symbols, emojis, and so on

▲ ***Figure 4*** *Features of ASCII and Unicode*

REVISION TIP 

You won't need to remember any ASCII codes. If you are told the code of one letter (for example, 'A') you can work out other letter codes by just counting through the alphabet.

There are different versions of ASCII and Unicode. The exact number of bits or bytes per character can vary.

Use summary units

You already know the meaning of bit, byte, and nibble. File size is counted in bytes. Often, files have millions or billions of bytes.

Instead of writing large values you can use summary units, shown in **Figure 5.**

Unit	Abbreviation	Size
Kilobyte	KB	1000 bytes
Megabyte	MB	1000 KB
Gigabyte	GB	1000 MB
Terabyte	TB	1000 GB
Petabyte	PB	1000 TB

▲ ***Figure 5*** *Summary units*

Converting	Calculation	Example
KB into MB	Divide by 1000	4000 KB ÷ 1000 = 4 MB
MB into KB	Multiply by 1000	1.25 MB × 1000 = 1250 KB

▲ ***Figure 6*** *Conversion between units*

To convert between units you either divide or multiply by 1000. Some examples are shown in **Figure 6**.

Calculate file size in bits

To calculate the size of a file you need to multiply two values. These are:

- the number of data points in the file
- the number of bits used for each data point.

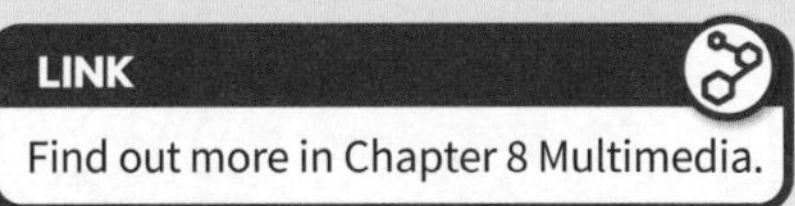
LINK
Find out more in Chapter 8 Multimedia.

Type of data	Calculation	Helpful hint	Example
Text	number of characters × bits per character	The number of bits per character can vary according to the version of ASCII or Unicode in use.	A text file that is 500 characters long with 16 bits per character would have a file size of 8000 bits = 1000 bytes = 1 KB.
Image	number of pixels × colour depth	Find number of pixels by multiplying image height by image width, both measured in pixels.	An image that is 200 × 300 pixels and has a colour depth of 16 bits would have a file size of 960 000 bits = 120 000 bytes = 120 KB.
Sound	number of seconds × sample rate in hertz × bit depth	Bit depth is the number of bits used per sound sample.	A 2-minute audio file with a sample rate of 44.1kHz (44 100 hertz) and a bit depth of 16 would have a file size of 84 672 000 bits = 10 584 000 bytes = 10.6 MB.

▲ ***Figure 7*** *Calculating file sizes*

This gives the number of bits in the file. You may need to divide by 8 to get the number of bytes.

Knowledge

9 File size

Metadata

Some image files have extra information as well as the pixels. This is called **metadata**.

Metadata stores additional image information, such as the size or shape of the image.

Some images have a text caption to help those who are visually impaired. Metadata adds a little bit extra to the image file size.

Worked example 1

A text file holds 30 000 Unicode characters. The version of Unicode uses 32 bits per character. How big is the file in bytes? Use a suitable binary unit.

To calculate the size of a text file:

- multiply number of characters by bits per character
- divide by 8 to convert bits into bytes
- convert to the simplest binary units.

30 000 × 32 = 960 000 bits — The number of characters and the bits per character are given in the question.

960 000 ÷ 8 = 120 000 bytes — Divide by 8 to give bytes.

120 000 bytes = 120 KB — Because the answer is between one thousand and one million bytes, convert it to kilobytes.

Worked example 2

A sound file holds 30 seconds of music at a sample rate of 46 000 Hz and a bit depth of 16. What is the total file size in bytes? Give the answer using suitable units.

To calculate the size of a sound file:

- multiply seconds by sample rate by bit depth
- divide by 8 to convert bits into bytes
- convert to the simplest binary units.

30 × 46 000 × 16 = 22 080 000 bits — The number of seconds, the sample rate, and the bit depth are all given in the question.

22 080 000 ÷ 8 = 2 760 000 bytes — The answer is in bits. Divide by 8 to give the number of bytes.

2 760 000 bytes = 2.76 MB — Because the answer is several million bytes, convert it to megabytes.

Compression

It is sometimes possible to reduce the size of a file. This called compression. There are two types of compression.

- **Lossy compression:** the file gets smaller, but there is a loss of quality (for example, sound quality).
- **Lossless compression:** sometimes it is possible to compress a file without loss of quality, but the reduction in file size may be less than with lossy compression.

A compressed file takes up less storage space. It can be quicker to transmit – for example, over an internet connection.

REVISION TIP 

Compression doesn't mean that bits are sent more quickly. It means fewer bits are needed to represent digital content.

REVISION TIP 

Lossy Compression means some data will be lost (deleted) when compressed.

LINK

Find out more in Chapter 11 Standards and protocols.

Key terms
Make sure you can write a definition for these key terms.

ASCII lossy compression lossless compression metadata Unicode

Retrieval

Learn the answers to the questions below, then cover the answers column with a piece of paper and write down as many answers as you can. Check and repeat.

	Questions	Answers
1	What are the advantages and disadvantages of ASCII compared to Unicode?	ASCII uses less storage space for each character, but it has a more restricted character set than Unicode
2	What are the advantages and disadvantages of Unicode compared to ASCII?	Unicode has a much greater range of characters than ASCII but it uses more storage space for each character
3	How would you calculate the amount of storage space needed for an ASCII file?	to store an ASCII file you need 1 byte for every character in the file
4	If a file size was greater than 1 000 KB, how would you change it to make sure it is shown in the most suitable units?	if a file size is greater than 1000 KB then divide by 1000 and show the size in megabytes (MB)
5	List the binary units greater than 1 MB, giving the size and abbreviation of each.	gigabyte GB = 1000 MB; terabyte TB = 1000 GB; petabyte PB = 1000 TB
6	How do you calculate the number of pixels in an image?	number of pixels in an image = height of image in pixels × width of image in pixels
7	If you know the number of pixels in an image, how do you calculate the file size in bits?	multiply the number of pixels by the colour depth (the number of bits per pixel)
8	What three factors must you multiply together to find the size of a sound file?	the number of seconds, the sample rate per second, and the bit depth
9	What is metadata and how does it change the size of an image file?	metadata stores additional image information; this increases the size of an image file
10	What are the advantages and disadvantages of lossless compression compared to lossy compression?	lossless compression reduces file size with no loss of data quality; however, it does not reduce the file size as much as lossy compression does

Put paper here

Put paper here

Put paper here

Put paper here

Previous questions

Now go back and use the questions below to check your knowledge from previous chapters.

	Previous questions	Answers
1	How is sample rate linked to sound quality?	the more often the sound is sampled, the better the quality of the sound
2	What is meant by the bit depth of a sound recording?	the number of codes available to record the different sounds
3	Explain why using virtual memory makes the computer go more slowly.	it takes longer for the computer to fetch data and instructions from storage that it does from RAM
4	Explain why RAM is called 'volatile' memory.	because the content of the memory is lost if the power is interrupted
5	State the full name and abbreviation for the three parts of the processor.	memory unit – RAM; control unit – CU; arithmetic/logic unit – ALU

Put paper here

Put paper here

Practice

Exam-style questions

1 Tick (✓) **one** box in each row to identify the binary unit equivalent of each of the given file sizes.

File size	4 megabytes	4 kilobytes	4 petabytes	4 gigabytes	4 terabytes
4000 terabytes					
4000 megabytes					
4000 gigabytes					
8000 nibbles					

[4]

2 An 8-bit colour depth image is 480 pixels wide by 640 pixels high.

Calculate the file size of the image in kilobytes. Show your working. **[3]**

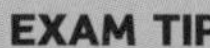

EXAM TIP

A conversion factor of 1000 is generally assumed for calculations or conversions, but 1024 is also acceptable.

3 The binary number 0101 0000 is used to represent the letter P using the ASCII character set.

Identify the character that would be represented by the denary number 85. Show your working. **[2]**

EXAM TIP

Binary representation of ASCII in the exam will use 8 bits.

4 A student wishes to compress their computer program file to send it to a teacher by email.

Explain why lossy compression would not be a suitable form of compression to compress the computer program file. **[3]**

EXAM TIP

Make notes of the points you want to make and tick them off as you work through your answer.

Knowledge

10 Networks

Computer connections

Computers can share digital data with other computers. Digital connections let computers share data in digital form (as numbers made of on–off signals). When computers are joined with digital connections, we call that a **network**.

LINK

Find out more in Chapter 7 Storing data.

There is more than one way to send signals between computers.

Signals travel through the **transmission media**.

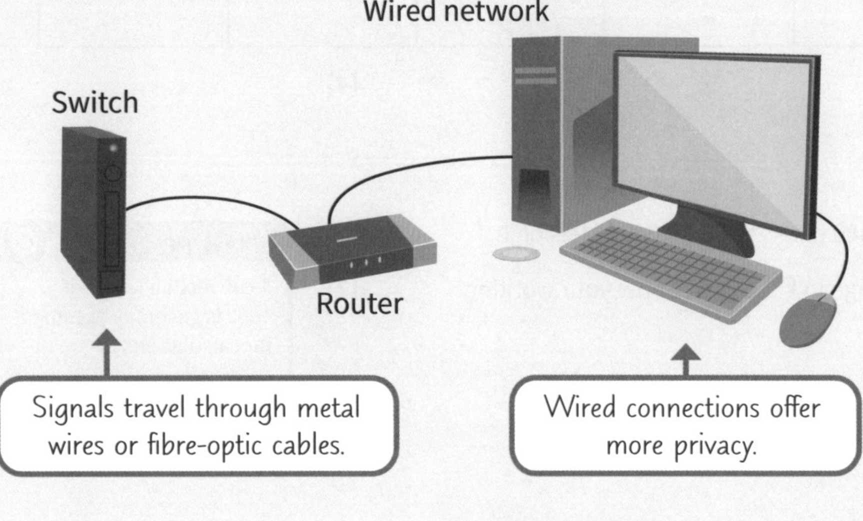

Wired network
Switch
Router
Signals travel through metal wires or fibre-optic cables.
Wired connections offer more privacy.

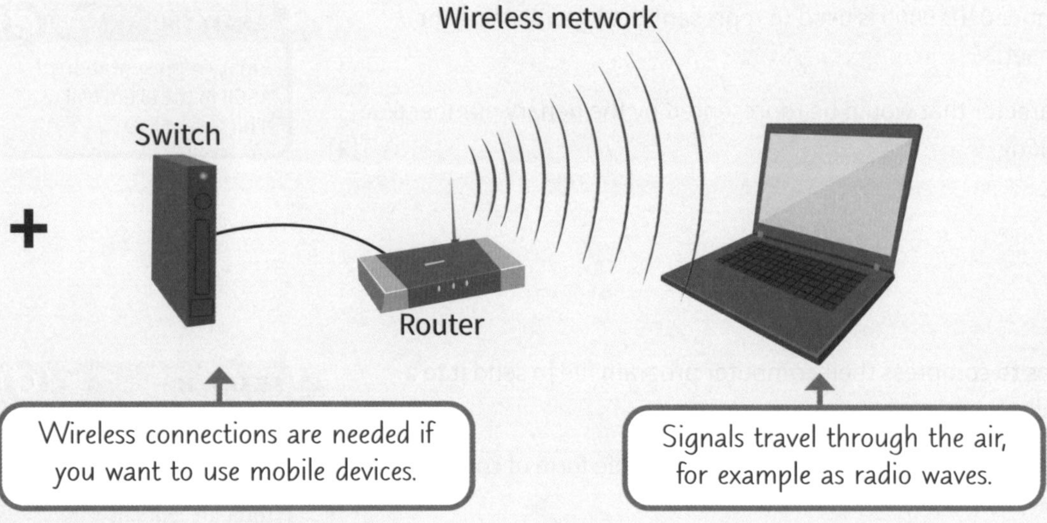

Wireless network
Switch
+
Router
Wireless connections are needed if you want to use mobile devices.
Signals travel through the air, for example as radio waves.

▲ ***Figure 1*** *Wired and wireless networks*

Key terms **Make sure you can write a definition for these key terms.**

bandwidth client–server local area network (LAN) mesh topology network network interface controller (NIC) peer-to-peer router star topology switch transmission media wide area network (WAN) wireless access point (WAP)

LANs and WANs

Networks can join computers that are close to each other (a **local area network**, or **LAN**), or far apart (a **wide area network**, or **WAN**).

Type of network	Abbreviation	Description	Type of connection	Example
Local area network	LAN	Joins computers on the same site or building.	Uses cables or wireless owned and used by a single organisation.	The network in your office or school.
Wide area network	WAN	Joins computers on different sites, cities, or countries.	Uses shared transmission media such as publicly owned cables.	The network that connects the ATM in a village to a bank in a distant city.

▲ ***Figure 2*** *LANs and WANs*

REVISION TIP 

Be prepared to respond to scenarios or case studies in which you will have to choose the right network solution. All the details you need will be in the question – read it carefully.

Understand: Network shapes

Networks can be different shapes. Different network shapes are called **topologies**. Two key topologies are **star** and **mesh** networks.

A star network is quicker and easier to set up.

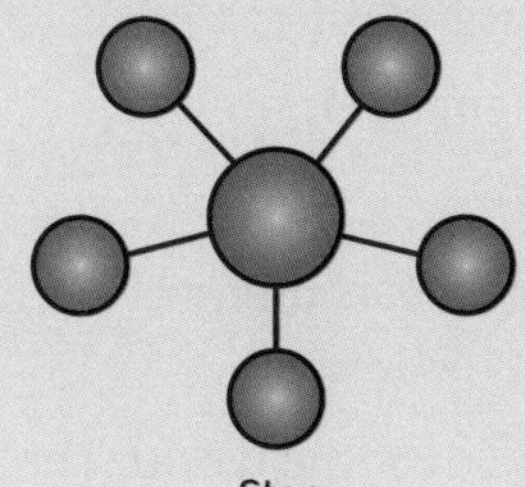

In a star network each computer is joined to a central device. All connections go through the centre.

A mesh network is more stable – even if some connections break, the network still works.

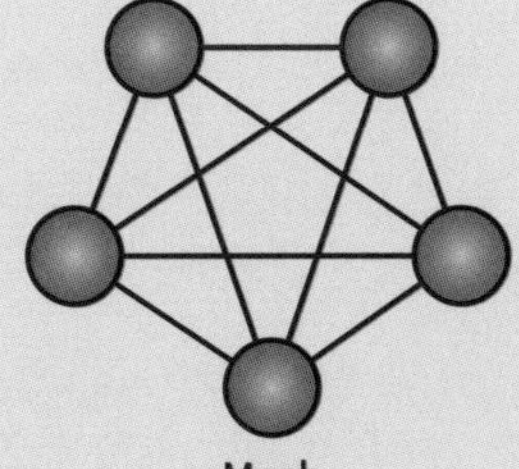

In a mesh network there is no central point. There are many different ways through the network.

▲ ***Figure 3*** *Star and mesh networks*

10 Networks

Peers and clients

The relationship between the computers in a network can be equal or unequal. Equal relationships are called **peer-to-peer**. Unequal relationships are called **client–server**.

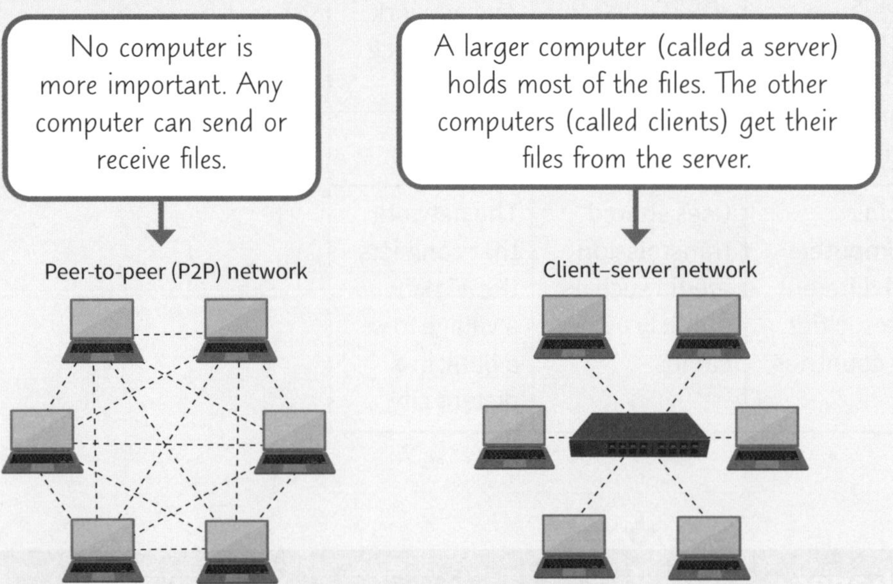

No computer is more important. Any computer can send or receive files.
A larger computer (called a server) holds most of the files. The other computers (called clients) get their files from the server.
Peer-to-peer (P2P) network
Client–server network

▲ ***Figure 4*** *Peer-to-peer and client–server networks*

There are many types of server. For example:

- A file server stores files for the client computers.
- An email server sends and receives emails for the client computers.
- A printer server sends files to a printer.
- A web server provides content such as a web page through an internet connection.

The internet is a mesh network that connects devices all over the world. The devices can communicate because they all use the same communication protocols.

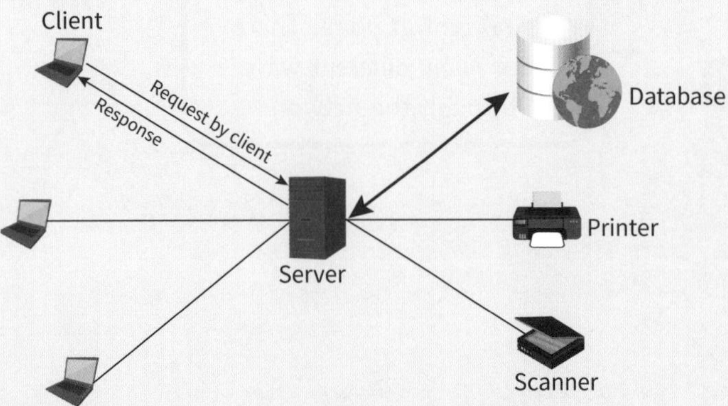

▲ ***Figure 5*** *The structure of a client–server network*

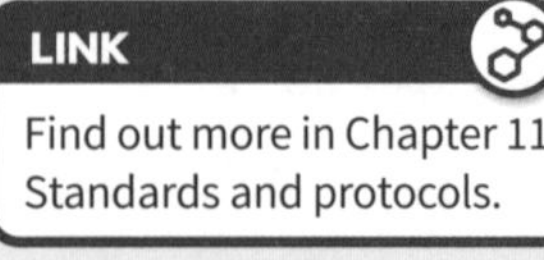

REVISION TIP

Remember: a server computer *provides* services. A client computer *uses* those services.

Network hardware

To make a network you need several different items of hardware:

- **Wireless access points (WAP):** sends out signals such as radio waves, to make a wireless connection.
- **Switch:** connects several computers, for example in a star network. It checks each message and sends it to the correct computer.
- **Router:** connects one network to another, for example your school network to the internet.
- **NIC (network interface controller):** The electrical components inside a computer that let it send and receive network signals.

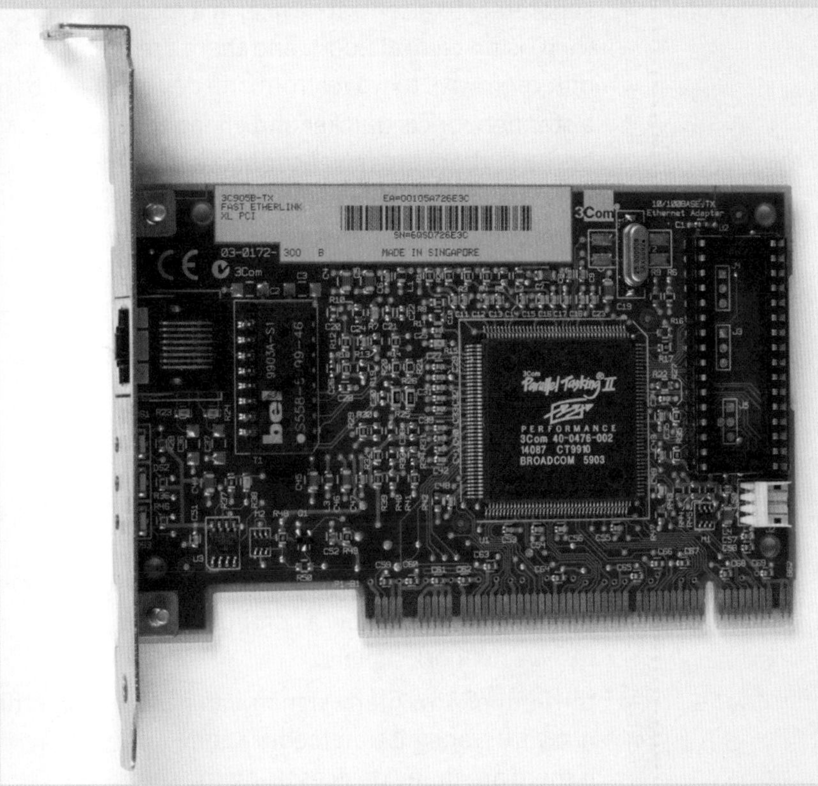

▲ *Figure 6 NIC components can be on a separate card, included as part of the main computer, or on a plug-in USB device*

REVISION TIP 

Make notes to help you remember the tasks performed by each piece of hardware.

Network performance

Just like computers, networks can have better or worse performance. A high performance network gives you a fast connection.

There is a limit to how many signals can travel through the transmission media at one time. This is the **bandwidth** of the network connection. If there are a lot of devices using the network you need more bandwidth.

If there isn't enough bandwidth, or there are too many devices, the network will slow down.

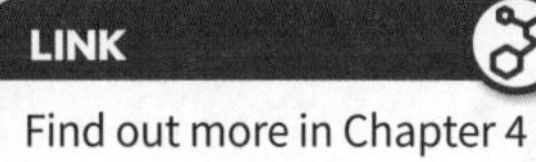

LINK

Find out more in Chapter 4 The Processor.

Retrieval

Learn the answers to the questions below, then cover the answers column with a piece of paper and write down as many answers as you can. Check and repeat.

	Questions	Answers
1	What are the key features of a local area network (LAN)?	a LAN links computers on the same site; communication is through privately-owned transmission media, used by a single organisation
2	What are the features of a wide area network (WAN)?	a WAN links computers on different sites, often far apart; communication is through shared transmission media such as publicly owned cables
3	What is the difference between the topology of a star and a mesh network?	in a star network each computer is connected separately to a central device; in a mesh network there is no central point, and there are many different ways to travel from one device to another
4	What are the different advantages of the star and mesh topologies?	a star network is quicker and cheaper to set up because there are fewer connections; a mesh network is less likely to fail because there are many ways through the network
5	What are the key features of a peer-to-peer network?	the computers in the network are of equal importance, and files can be held on any computer
6	What are the key features of a client–server network?	one computer, the server, holds the key files, and provides them to the client computers
7	Give three key types of server in a client–server network.	file server, email server, web server
8	Give the function of each of these key items of network hardware; wireless access point, switch, router, NIC (network interface controller).	allows a device to make a wireless connection to a network; sends network signals on to the correct device; connects two networks; holds the electronic components that allow a computer to send and receive network signals
9	What is meant by bandwidth?	the limit of how many signals can pass through the network transmission media at one time
10	How can bandwidth affect network performance?	if there are many devices using the same connection, or sending and receiving large files, then the connection can slow down

Put paper here

Previous questions

Now go back and use the questions below to check your knowledge from previous chapters.

	Previous questions	Answers
1	List the binary units greater than 1 MB, giving the size and abbreviation of each.	gigabyte GB = 1 000 MB; terabyte TB = 1000 GB; petabyte PB = 1000 TB
2	How do you calculate the number of pixels in an image?	number of pixels in an image = height of image in pixels × width of image in pixels
3	Describe what virtual memory means.	when the computer runs out of space in memory, it moves some instructions and data to storage
4	What is stored in ROM?	the start-up instructions for the computer

Put paper here

Exam-style questions

1 A router is a piece of hardware that can be used to connect stand-alone computers into a Local Area Network (LAN).

Identify **three** hardware items needed to connect stand-alone computers into a LAN. **[3]**

2 Describe **two** factors that can affect the performance of a network. **[4]**

EXAM TIP

Write your answers clearly. If an examiner cannot read what you have written you may not get the full marks available.

3 Mesh is a network topology.

Give **two** benefits and **two** drawbacks of a mesh network. **[4]**

EXAM TIP

Practice drawing network topology diagrams. They can help you answer some network questions.

11 Standards and protocols

Setting common standards

Common **standards** are rules for how computers work. Different companies make hardware and software. However, they all use the same standards because they need their devices to be able to work together. For example, the design of a USB connection is a common standard.

A **protocol** is a standard for communication. Protocols set the rules for how signals are sent through network connections.

Standards for transmission media

You have learned that networks can use wired or wireless connections. These are the transmission media.

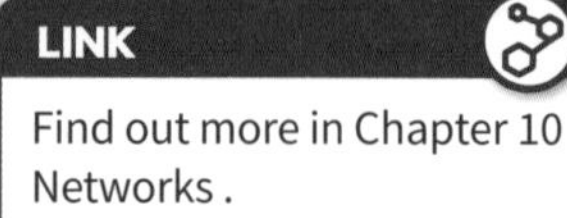

LINK

Find out more in Chapter 10 Networks .

The most often used standards for transmission media are **ethernet**, **Wi-Fi** and **Bluetooth**.

Ethernet is a standard for connecting computers to a network using a cable. **Figure 1** shows an ethernet connection.

Wi-Fi is a standard for sending and receiving wireless signals. If a device uses the Wi-Fi standard it can pick up a network signal in any Wi-Fi hotspot. Almost all wireless devices can do this.

Bluetooth is a standard for communication with devices that are nearby. For example, you can use Bluetooth to connect wireless headphones to your laptop.

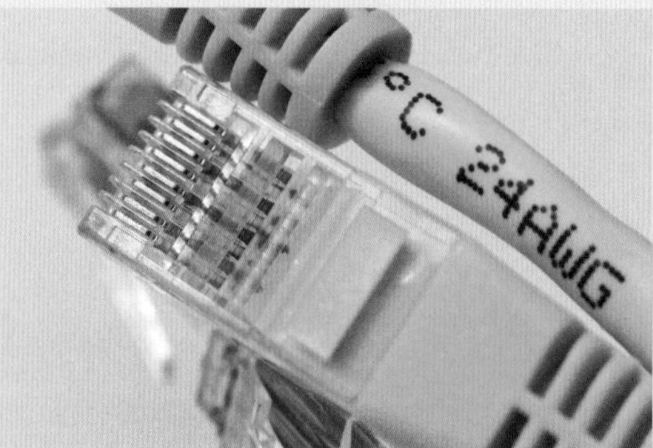

▲ ***Figure 1*** *Ethernet connects devices in LAN and WAN*

▲ ***Figure 2*** *Wi-Fi allows devices to interface with the internet*

▲ ***Figure 3*** *Bluetooth is a short range wireless technology*

REVISION TIP

Make notes on the benefit of wireless versus wired connections.

Internet protocols

The internet facilitates lots of computers working together to send and receive messages. There are many **protocols** involved. Protocols are standards for communication.

Abbreviation	Full name	What is it for?
TCP/IP	Transmission control protocol/ internet protocol	These two protocols work together to control the journey of a message through the internet to the right address
HTTP	Hyper text transfer protocol	This protocol lets us send web pages through the internet
HTTPS	Hyper text transfer protocol secure	The same as HTTP but with extra security checks in place (see below)
FTP	File transfer protocol	This protocol lets us send files from computer to computer in a client-server network

▲ ***Figure 4*** *Common internet protocols*

If a web page uses the HTTPS protocol it is more secure. The signals to and from the web page are encrypted. The web page has been checked to confirm it is what it claims to be.

▶ ***Figure 5*** *In most browsers the HTTPS protocol is shown by a padlock symbol*

REVISION TIP

For your GCSE exam, you don't need to know how the different protocols and standards work. However, you must understand why society need protocols and standards. Make sure you are able to give examples.

Email protocols

There are also protocols to allow email communication.

Abbreviation	Full name	What is it for?
POP	Post office protocol	Moves our emails from an email server onto our own computer
IMAP	Internet message access protocol	A more modern email protocol; lets us look at our emails on an internet page
SMTP	Simple mail transfer protocol	Sends email messages to other computers

▲ ***Figure 6*** *Common email protocols*

REVISION TIP 

Make sure you can outline the purpose and key features of the basic principles of each protocol.

Knowledge

11 Standards and protocols

Protocol layers

When a message is sent through the internet, it has to use many protocols. The different protocol signals are added to the message before it is sent. They are stacked on top of each other in layers.

The message is passed from computer to computer on an internet journey. When the message gets to its destination the layers of protocol are removed in reverse order.

Addresses

Every device in a network must have its own address. This makes sure messages and signals go to the right address.

- Every single digital device has its own **MAC address**. MAC stands for media access control. The MAC address is added in the factory when the device is made. Because of the MAC address, signals on a local network can go to the right device.
- Every device with an internet connection has an **IP address**. IP stands for internet protocol. The IP address is a large number. The IP address is used to send signals on the internet to the right destination.

The original type of IP address used 32 bits (4 bytes). This is called IPv4. However, the internet got so big that more numbers were needed. The modern address system is called IPv6. This uses 128 bits (16 bytes).

LINK 

Find out more in Chapter 7 Storing data.

REVISION TIP 

Understand IP addressing and the formatting of an IP address (IPv4 and IPv6).

```
Wireless LAN adapter Wi-Fi 2:

   Connection-specific DNS Suffix  . :
   Description . . . . . . . . . . . : Qualcomm QCA9565 802.11b/g/n Wireless Adapter #2
   Physical Address. . . . . . . . . : 80-2B-F9-A6-A1-E3
   DHCP Enabled. . . . . . . . . . . : Yes
   Autoconfiguration Enabled . . . . : Yes
   Link-local IPv6 Address . . . . . : fe80::4e70:c403:17ba:5404%18(Preferred)
   IPv4 Address. . . . . . . . . . . : 192.168.0.110(Preferred)
```

The IP address is shown in both IPv4 and IPv6 forms. IPv6 is longer.

DHCP is one of the many protocols that help devices communicate.

The physical address is the MAC address of the object.

▲ ***Figure 7*** *Address information for a typical wireless adapter*

The internet

An IP address is a large number. The numbers are difficult for human users to read and use. As well as an IP address, every internet device has a **domain name**. This uses text to identify every web resource, such as a web page. The standard system for linking each domain name to the right IP addresses is called the domain name system (DNS).

A computer with a full-time internet connection is called a **web server**. Web pages are held on web servers. When a server holds a web page, it is called **web hosting**. Every web server will have its own IP address and domain name.

If you use the internet, at work or school, for example, you probably don't have your own internet connection. You connect through a web server or router that has its own IP address and domain name.

LINK

Find out more in Chapter 10 Networks.

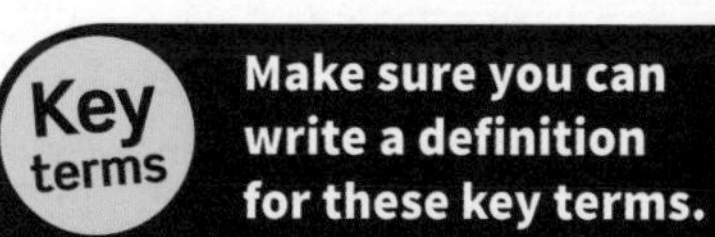
Key
terms
Make sure you can
write a definition
for these key terms.

Bluetooth domain name ethernet IP address
MAC address protocol web hosting web server Wi-Fi

Retrieval

Learn the answers to the questions below, then cover the answers column with a piece of paper and write down as many answers as you can. Check and repeat

	Questions	Answers
1	What are standards and why are they needed by computers?	standards are agreed ways of doing things so that devices made by different manufacturers can work together
2	Describe the three common standards for transmission media.	ethernet for connecting computers to a network by a plugged-in cable; Wi-Fi for connecting a device to a local wireless network; Bluetooth for connecting personal devices wirelessly over a short distance
3	What is a protocol?	a protocol is a standard for communication
4	What protocols are involved in sending and receiving emails?	POP, IMAP, SMTP
5	What other protocols are used to allow internet connections?	TCP/IP, HTTP, HTTPS, FTP
6	What are protocol layers and when are they used?	when a message is sent through the internet, protocols are added in layers before the message is sent out; they are removed in reverse order when the message arrives
7	What is the difference between a MAC address and an IP address?	a MAC address identifies an individual device; an IP address identifies an internet location
8	Explain the difference between IPv4 and IPv6.	IP addresses are held as binary numbers; IPv4 uses 32 bits for each number; IPv6 uses 128 bits so there are far more numbers available
9	Explain how a domain name is related to an IP address.	domain names are a way of identifying web resources using text instead of numbers; every device with an internet connection has a domain name as well as an IP address
10	What is web hosting?	when a web server – a computer with a permanent connection to the internet – holds web pages that can be accessed through an internet connection

Put paper here

Previous questions

Now go back and use the questions below to check your knowledge from previous chapters.

	Previous questions	Answers
1	What is the difference between the topology of a star and a mesh network?	in a star network each computer is connected separately to a central device; in a mesh network there is no central point, and there are many different ways to travel from one device to another
2	What are the key features of a client–server network?	one computer, the server, holds the key files, and provides them to the client computers

Put paper here

Practice

Exam-style questions

1 Outline the purpose of the domain name service (DNS). **[1]**

2 Every device on the internet has an internet protocol (IP) address and a media access control (MAC) address.

Identify **one** difference and **one** similarity between IP and MAC addresses. **[2]**

EXAM TIP 

If a difference or similarity between two items is needed, you must refer to both items to gain the marks.

3 Protocols are used when computers communicate with each other.

Explain why protocols are used. **[2]**

EXAM TIP 

For your GCSE exam, you don't need to know how the different protocols and standards work. However, you should understand why we need protocols and standards and be able to name some examples and why they are used.

4 Identify and describe **three** email protocols. **[6]**

EXAM TIP

Remember to use technical terms and abbreviations accurately.

12 Online security

Access to data

A network is typically used by many users. The users can share data files and software. However, just because you are on a network doesn't mean you can access all the files on the network.

Different user access levels	
No access	You can't even view the files
Read-only access	You can view the files ('read' them) but not change them
Read-write access	You can view files and make changes to them

You may have different levels of access to different files. Most users have a **password**. The password proves your identity when you log on to the network. That gives you access to the files you are allowed to work with.

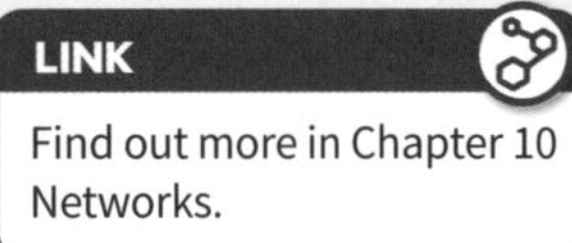

Find out more in Chapter 10 Networks.

Security risks

There is a risk that data may be accessed by people who should not be able to see or alter it. This can be a risk to both privacy and security. It can lead to theft and fraud.

Key ways to attack systems include:

- Causing loss and damage: data, software or even digital hardware can be damaged on purpose. People might do this for a joke or to cause harm.
- Finding out passwords: if you find out someone's password you can log in as them and access their data.
- Intercepting messages: reading or copying data as it passes through the transmission media.

Wireless transmission can be less secure than cable transmission. Anyone with a wireless connection can pick up the signals. To prevent people intercepting messages, you can use **encryption**.

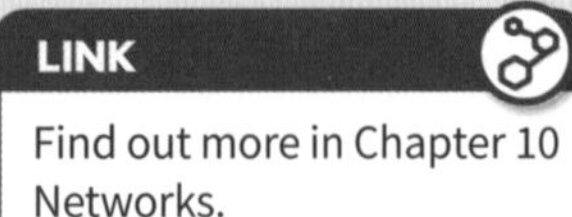

Find out more in Chapter 10 Networks.

Finding out passwords

Passwords are essential for gaining access to data files.

There are two key ways for hackers to find out a password:

- Brute force: this means trying every possible combination of words and numbers until you get the right password by chance.
- **Social engineering**: this means tricking people into telling you their password. For example, someone might pretend to be a lottery company and say that you need to provide your banking details so they can give you a prize.

Tricking people by using a pretend email is called **phishing**.

Tricking people by using a pretend website is called **pharming**.

You can protect yourself from these tricks. Use uncommon passwords that are harder to guess and include lower case and upper case letters, numbers and characters. Never share your password.

REVISION TIP 

Consider how these attacks are used and why they are used.

Malware

Malware is short for malicious software. The most common type of malware is a computer virus.

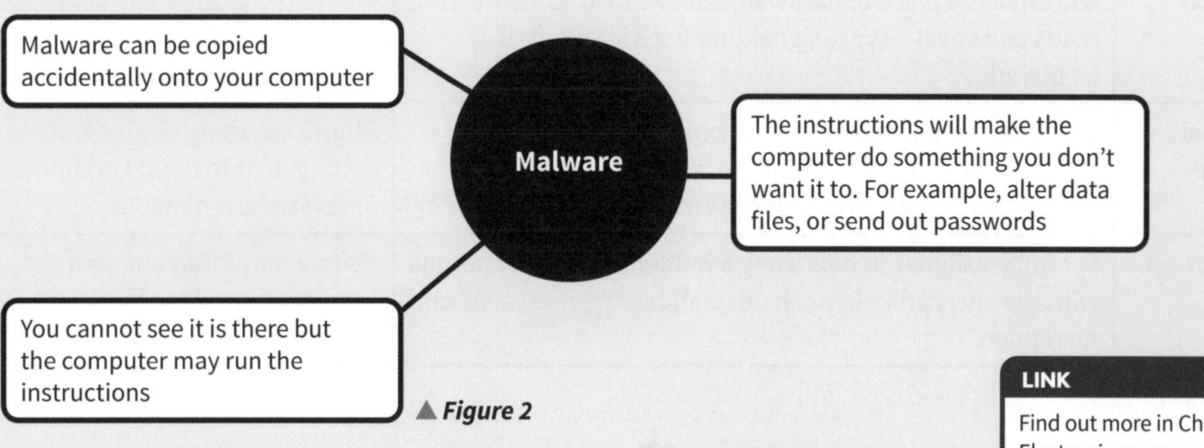

Malware can be copied accidentally onto your computer
Malware
The instructions will make the computer do something you don't want it to. For example, alter data files, or send out passwords
You cannot see it is there but the computer may run the instructions

▲ *Figure 2*

LINK

Find out more in Chapter 5 Electronic memory.

You can buy and install anti-malware software. This software will check your emails and files for hidden malware instructions. It will delete the malware.

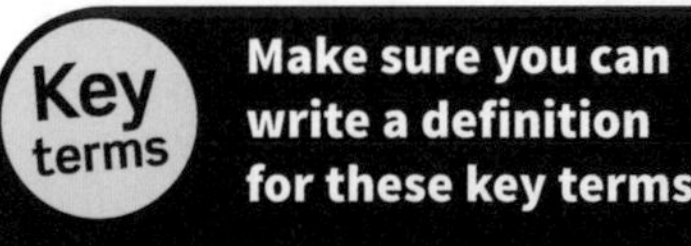

Make sure you can write a definition for these key terms.

biometrics denial of service encryption firewall hackers malware password pharming phishing read–write access read-only access social engineering SQL injection user access levels

12 Online security

Other threats

Other threats can have the effect of damaging computer systems:

Denial of service (also called DoS or DDoS): hackers try to stop a computer network from working. They send massive amounts of messages or requests to the network. The aim is to overload the server or the bandwidth.

SQL injection: SQL means 'structured query language'. Commands in SQL can be used to edit or delete data in a database. If you put an SQL command into the data of a database, that can make the database delete its own files.

LINK

Find out more in Chapter 10 Networks.

LINK

Find out more in Chapter 33 Data tables.

How to protect data

As well as protecting your information with passwords and anti-malware software, there are other methods to improve security.

Protection	How it works	Aim of the protection
Penetration testing	People who have permission from the owners try to break into a secure network. They hope to find out the weak points	Tests a computer system to find security weaknesses
Firewall	A firewall is a piece of hardware with its own software. It reads and checks every signal that goes in or out of a network	Prevents malware and other harmful content from getting onto a network
Physical security	Computers are kept in locked rooms. There are security staff on guard. Entry to the room is controlled by passcodes, swipe cards, or **biometrics** (e.g. a thumbprint)	Stops the wrong people from getting near to digital equipment or transmission media
Encryption	Scrambles digital signals using a hidden code. Only people with the encryption key can unscramble the messages and read them	People may intercept your messages but they cannot read them

▲ ***Figure 3*** *Methods to improve security*

How to protect data

▲ ***Figure 4*** *Thumbprints and retinal scans are examples of biometric security*

Before you send personal information to a web page, make sure it uses the HTTPS protocol. That means the web page uses encryption. The owner of the web page has been checked and it is not a trick or a scam.

LINK

Find out more in Chapter 11 Standards and protocols.

REVISION TIP

Be aware of the principles of each type of protection. For example, encryption does not stop data theft, it only protects the data from being read easily.

Retrieval

Learn the answers to the questions below, then cover the answers column with a piece of paper and write down as many answers as you can. Check and repeat.

Questions		Answers
1 Describe the three user access levels.	Put paper here	read–write access: see and change files; read-only access: see files but can't make changes; no access: can't see files
2 What is the brute force method for finding out a password?		try every combination of characters until you hit the right password by chance
3 What is the social engineering method for finding out a password?	Put paper here	trick someone into telling you their password, for example by pretending to be a legitimate organisation like a bank
4 What is malware and why does it pose a threat to computer systems?		malware is malicious software you can't see on your computer; the computer will run the software and do something that you don't want it to do
5 How does a denial of service attack disrupt a computer system?	Put paper here	too many messages or requests are sent to a computer system; they overload the server or the bandwidth
6 What is SQL injection?		SQL is a programming language used to work with databases; if you put an SQL command into the data of a database, that can make the database delete its own files
7 Explain how penetration testing is used to make a system more secure.	Put paper here	people try to break into a computer system to find weaknesses in the system and get past the security; they have permission from the system owners
8 What is a firewall and how does it protect a computer system?		a firewall is made of hardware and software; it reads and checks every signal that goes in to or out of a network to stop harmful content
9 Describe three physical security methods.	Put paper here	rooms are physically locked; security staff on guard; entry to the room is controlled by, for example, passcodes, swipe cards, or biometrics
10 How does encrypting your messages help to protect them from unauthorised access?		encryption scrambles digital signals using a hidden code; intercepted messages can't be read

Previous questions

Now go back and use the questions below to check your knowledge from previous chapters.

Previous questions		Answers
1 Explain the difference between IPv4 and IPv6.	Put paper here	IP addresses are held as binary numbers; IPv4 uses 32 bits for each number; IPv6 uses 128 bits so there are far more numbers available
2 Explain how a domain name is related to an IP address.		domain names are a way of identifying web resources using text instead of numbers; every device with an internet connection has a domain name as well as an IP address

Practice

Exam-style questions

1 Describe how encryption is used to secure data that is transmitted across a network. [3]

> **EXAM TIP**
> When answering questions on encryption, choose your words carefully. Encrypted files can still be accessed, altered, and deleted.

2 Explain how a denial of service attack is used to disrupt the operation of a web server. [3]

> **EXAM TIP**
> Questions with an * as part of the question number are essay questions and require answers to be written in continuous prose in standard English.

3* Computer systems use different methods to protect data from theft and interception.

Discuss the positive and negative aspects of a range of protection methods to prevent data theft and interception, including:

- encryption
- firewalls
- passwords. [8]

> **EXAM TIP**
> A discussion requires both positive and negative statements.

> **EXAM TIP**
> Make sure you include any specific items listed in the question in your answer.

13 Social issues

Digital technology

Digital means 'made of numbers'. **Digital technology** means any device that processes data in number form. Of course that includes computers, but also laptops, phones, cameras, tablets, and other devices with embedded processors.

New digital technologies are being invented all the time. Some may be so new that they do not appear in text books and revision guides. All types of technology can have an impact on our lives.

LINK 

Find out more in Chapter 6 Operating systems.

Technology and ethics

Ethics means the rules of right and wrong. Our ideas about right and wrong can arise from shared cultural and religious beliefs, and from our own reflections and thoughts. How we use technology is affected by ethical issues, just like every other part of life.

REVISION TIP 

To reflect on technology and ethics, you should think about your own values. You should listen to people with different values, and think about what they say.

Ethical issues linked to technology

- New ways to harm others, such as bullying with online messages
- Loss of privacy
- Exposure to harmful content, such as political extremism and exploitation

REVISION TIP 

Questions on these topics will often be where the quality of your written communication is assessed.

These issues do not make technology bad. Digital technology is a tool like any other, which can be used to do good or cause harm.

Ethical benefits of technology

- Learning about different types of people, increasing our understanding and sympathy
- Bringing new opportunities for education and employment to people all over the world
- Finding people who share our values, and co-operating with them to bring about change
- Overcoming loneliness and social isolation

Knowledge

13 Social issues

Technology and privacy

Privacy is an important ethical consideration.

Technology gives people the power to read other people's messages. Signals can be intercepted as they pass through transmission media. Social media means that discussion between friends could be shared with strangers.

Governments and other organisations can use technology to monitor and control people, making it more difficult to be different or to disagree.

Technology can be used to protect privacy, but there are two important considerations:

- respect other people's privacy
- be aware of the risks – protect yourself by taking care when you share.

LINK 

Find out more in Chapter 12 Online security.

Technology and culture

Culture means the ideas and creations which enrich our society. It includes art, media and crafts and other valued activities.

Digital technology has an impact on culture by allowing:

- new forms of art and creativity, such as electronic music and video games
- the ability to mix and combine digital samples to create new art forms
- greater access to art and literature for people all over the world
- the ability to create and share our own art, as well as accessing other people's art
- a distraction from the things we value, wasting time in trivial ways

REVISION TIP 

Just like with ethics, technology can bring benefits or cause problems. You should understand both sides.

Technology and the environment

The **environment** means the natural world: the biological and physical world in which we live.

Damage to the environment can harm the health and prosperity of communities. A big consideration currently is climate change due to increased carbon dioxide (CO_2) in the atmosphere. CO_2 is released when fossil fuels are burned.

Pollution of air and water, and the destruction of animal habitats, are other areas of concern.

Technology does impact the environment, and once again there are good and bad aspects.

REVISION TIP 

You should be able to describe two or three ways in which technology brings benefits, and two or three ways in which it presents problems.

Building digital devices uses rare minerals. Mining for these minerals can cause pollution and destruction.	✗
Technology uses electricity. Some electricity is created by burning fossil fuels, releasing CO_2.	✗
Technology lets us work from home, and have meetings online. This is called remote working. Remote working means less travel, less pollution, less noise and congestion, and less use of fossil fuels.	✓
Technology helps scientists study the environment, to learn how to protect it.	✓

▲ ***Figure 1*** *Environmental problems and benefits of technology*

Digital technology enables us to do complicated calculations. Scientists can use technology to collect information about the environment. They can try to predict what will happen, to the climate for example. They may be able to invent solutions to our environmental problems.

▲ ***Figure 2*** *Manufacturing and mining contribute to pollution which in turn contributes to climate change and the impact that has on the environment*

REVISION TIP 

In many areas of technology, there are definite right and wrong answers. For example, when we are doing calculations there is a single right answer. Evaluating the impact of technology on social issues is different. Make sure you are aware of benefits and problems within each area. Provide examples of both in any discussion. and at the end of your answer, come to your own conclusion.

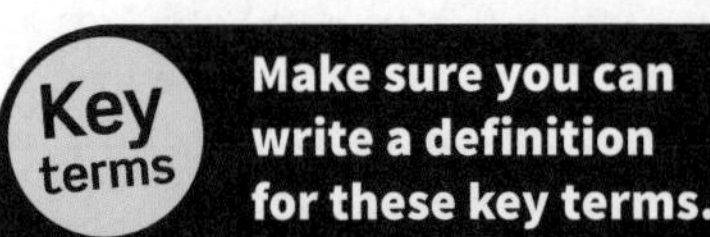

Make sure you can write a definition for these key terms.

cultural digital technology ethics environment privacy

Retrieval

Learn the answers to the questions below, then cover the answers column with a piece of paper and write down as many answers as you can. Check and repeat.

	Questions	Answers
1	What does ethical mean?	ethical means issues related to our values and beliefs about right and wrong
2	What ethical problems may be linked to digital technology?	new ways to cause harm such as digital bullying, exposure to harmful content, loss of privacy
3	What ethical benefits could arise from digital technology?	finding out about other types of people, co-operating with people who share our aims, bringing new opportunities, overcoming isolation
4	What new forms of culture have come into existence thanks to digital technology?	electronic music, video games, digital art made with computers, new ways of mixing and sampling art
5	Digital technology brings greater participation in art. Give reasons for and against this.	for: technology helps us make and share art, and gives greater access to art; against: it can be distracting so we don't concentrate or read as much
6	What is the environment?	the natural, physical, and biological world in which we live
7	Making and using digital devices can harm the environment. Give two ways this can happen.	mining for the rare minerals needed to make digital devices can harm the environment; digital devices use electricity which can be made by burning fossil fuels
8	Digital technology can enable remote working. What does that mean?	remote working means we can work from home and have meetings online instead of travelling to work or meeting face-to-face
9	How can remote working help the environment?	remote working means less travel, which means less pollution, less noise and congestion, and less use of fossil fuels
10	How could scientists use technology to help with environmental problems?	for example, collect information about the environment; make predictions; invent solutions to our environmental problems

Put paper here

Previous questions

Now go back and use the questions below to check your knowledge from previous chapters.

	Previous questions	Answers
1	What is malware and why does it pose a threat to computer systems?	malware is malicious software you can't see malware on your computer; the computer will run the software and do something that you don't want it to do
2	How does a denial of service attack disrupt a computer system?	too many messages or requests are sent to a computer system; they overload the server or the bandwidth

Put paper here

Exam-style questions

1 Identify **and** describe **one** benefit and **one** drawback of technology and its impact on the environment. **[4]**

EXAM TIP

This question asks for one benefit and one drawback. You should be able to describe two or three ways in which technology brings benefits, and two or three ways in which it brings problems.

2 Smart phones are an example of digital technology.

Outline **two** impacts of smart phones on the issue of privacy. **[4]**

3* Ethics means the rules of right and wrong. Our use of technology is affected by ethical issues, just like other aspects of life.

EXAM TIP

Spend a few minutes to plan and structure your answer. This will help you focus on the order of your answer and help you make all the points you want to make.

Evaluate the ethical issues linked to the use of technology. **[8]**

EXAM TIP

Some essay questions can use the 'evaluate' command word. To evaluate you need to:

- write about points that are benefits
- write about points that are drawbacks
- give your conclusion at the end.

Knowledge

14 Legal issues

Digital technology and the law

Laws are rules made by governments and are enforced by the police and the court system.

Many laws set out actions which are not allowed (prohibited). Some laws state actions that you must take (mandatory). The use of digital technology is affected by laws just like any other area of human life.

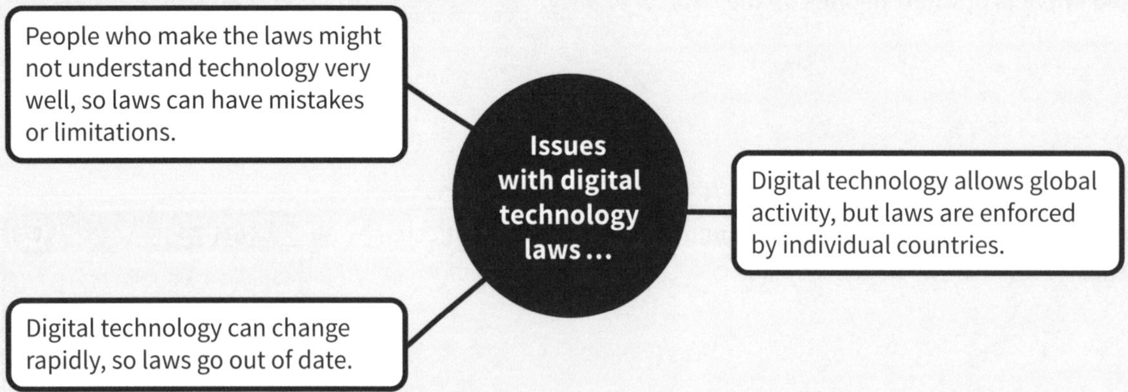

Issues with digital technology laws ...
People who make the laws might not understand technology very well, so laws can have mistakes or limitations.
Digital technology allows global activity, but laws are enforced by individual countries.
Digital technology can change rapidly, so laws go out of date.

Laws tend to be similar in different countries. Many countries have made agreements to align their laws regarding digital technology.

The laws featured and discussed in this section are all laws from the UK but there are similar laws in most countries.

Copyright Designs and Patents Act 1988

Whilst technology lets us make and share creative content such as music or computer games, it also makes it easier to copy creative content. People sometimes copy and sell digital content without permission from the person/people who made it. They do not pay for it.

LINK

Find out more in Chapter 13 Social issues.

The purpose of the Copyright Designs and Patents Act 1988 is to protect people who make and sell creative content. That includes digital content. If you make a piece of work, you have **copyright**. That means the rights to:

- decide who can copy or use the content
- be identified as the creator of the content
- get paid for use of the content.

Copyright is part of a larger set of rights called **intellectual property rights (IPR)**. This protection includes inventions, computer programs, and designs. If you work for a company, they may own the IPR or copyright of your work.

A small amount of copying or quoting is allowed, for example in education or in other art works. This is called 'fair dealing' in the UK (known as 'fair use' in the USA).

REVISION TIP

Make notes as you work through this section to help you remember the purpose of each piece of legislation and the specific actions it allows or prohibits.

Computer Misuse Act 1990

The Computer Misuse Act is the law introduced to prohibit hacking into other people's computers.

Hacking means getting round digital security measures. Hackers may read or change digital data held on computers. This can cause harm to privacy, or allow theft and sabotage.

LINK
Find out more in Chapter 12 Online security.

The definition of 'hacking' includes the spread of malware.

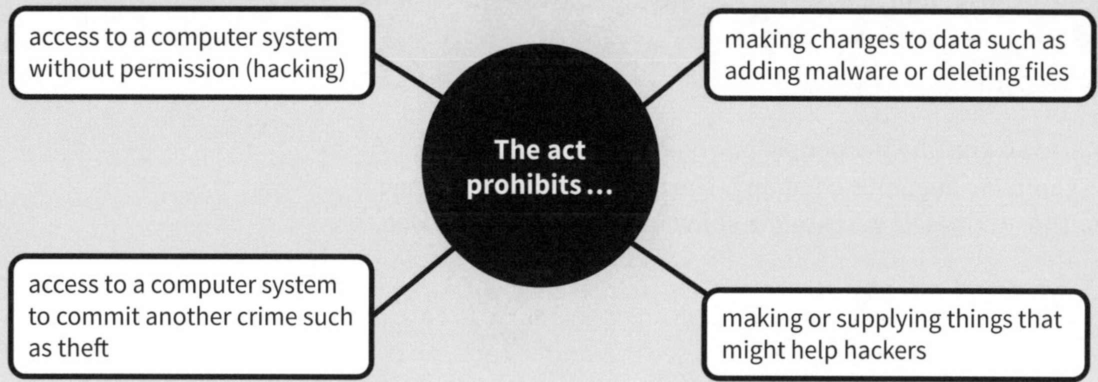
The act prohibits...
access to a computer system without permission (hacking)
making changes to data such as adding malware or deleting files
access to a computer system to commit another crime such as theft
making or supplying things that might help hackers

It can be hard to find and prosecute hackers because they are always developing new techniques to overcome security measures.

Data Protection Act 2018

The **Data Protection** Act in the UK was updated in 2018. It was updated in line with a Europe-wide agreement called **General Data Protection Regulation (GDPR)**. Most countries in and outside of Europe have similar laws.

The purpose of the law is to protect personal data. That means data that relates to individual people.

Legitimate reasons to hold data about you include agreed business transactions, and some other uses such as medical welfare and law enforcement.

The Data Protection Act 2018 means that:

- organisations are not allowed to collect and hold personal data except if it is necessary for a legitimate task (such as sending you a bill for something you bought) or you give permission
- they can't keep data once the need has finished
- if they have data, they must keep it safe and private, and not share it without permission; they must be as accurate as they can
- they must let you see the data they have about you, so you can check it
- if the data is wrong, they must change or delete it.

The person the data is about is called the data subject. The organisation that holds and uses the data is called the data controller.

Knowledge

14 Legal issues

Software licenses

Software means the instructions that control what a computer does. Computer games, apps, and utilities are examples of software. Software is covered by copyright laws.

Because software is easy to copy it is not usually offered for sale outright. Instead, you pay for a software **license**. Your license lets you use the software. Some licenses let a group of people use the software.

There are two main types of software license:

Proprietary software is owned by the people or organisation that made it, such as a software company or games company. The company makes money by selling licenses. The license lets you use the software. You are not allowed to make a copy.

Open-source software is usually free to use and copy. An open-source license lets you use the software without charge. It also lets you see the source code. That means the commands written in a programming language by the programmers. The source code is what makes the software work.

▲ ***Figure 1*** *Think about what open-source software you use and why you use it*

Open-source software may be improved and shared by lots of programmers. Nobody owns it. The programming language Python is an example of open-source software. It is the result of many programmers working for free and sharing their work.

LINK 

Find out more in Chapter 16 Writing algorithms.

REVISION TIP 

Make sure you can explain the difference between the features of open-source software and proprietary software. Note the key elements of each.

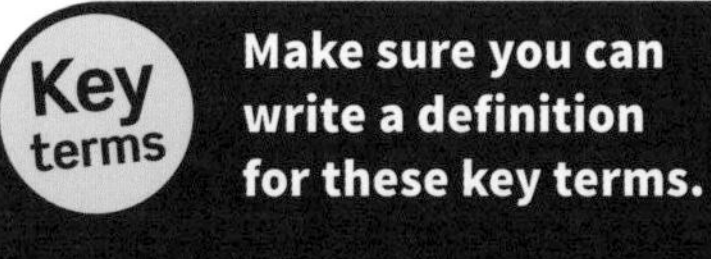

Key terms **Make sure you can write a definition for these key terms.**

copyright data protection
General Data Protection Regulation (GDPR)
intellectual property rights (IPR) license
open-source proprietary

Retrieval

Learn the answers to the questions below, then cover the answers column with a piece of paper and write down as many answers as you can. Check and repeat.

	Questions	Answers
1	Why are the main problems with making laws about digital technology?	mistakes or limitations because of lack of understanding; laws out of date because technology changes rapidly; laws within one country but digital technology allows global activity
2	What is copyright?	the right to decide who can use or copy creative content that you made
3	Why is copyright of digital content difficult to enforce?	because modern technology makes it very easy to make lots of copies of digital content
4	The Data Protection Act 2018 defines a 'data subject'. What is the data subject?	an individual person whose personal data is held on a computer system
5	An organisation can only hold data about you under limited circumstances. What are they?	you give permission or it is part of a legitimate task, for example an agreed business transaction such as a sale, and examples including medical treatment and law enforcement
6	What obligations does an organisation have to protect your personal data?	to hold the data with care and respect for your privacy; to be as accurate as possible; to give you the right to check and correct the data; to destroy the data when the legitimate use is over
7	What is a software license?	an agreement that you can make use of software; it usually includes payment and lasts for a set time only
8	What is proprietary software?	software that is owned by a company; you can only use it if you buy a license; you cannot make or sell copies
9	What is open-source software?	software that is developed and shared by a group of programmers; you can look at the commands; you can usually make changes and copies of the code

Put paper here

Previous questions

Now go back and use the questions below to check your knowledge from previous chapters.

	Previous questions	Answers
1	Making and using digital devices can harm the environment. Give two ways this can happen.	mining for rare minerals to make digital devices can harm the environment; digital devices use electricity made by burning fossil fuels
2	How can remote working help the environment?	remote working means less travel, which means less pollution, less noise and congestion, and less use of fossil fuels
3	What is a protocol?	a protocol is a standard for communication

Put paper here

Practice

Exam-style questions

1* A school keeps records of staff personal details on its computer system. The headteacher of the school wants to make sure that they fully comply with the Data Protection Act 2018.

Discuss the actions that the school should take to make sure it meets the requirements of the Data Protection Act 2018. **[8]**

EXAM TIP 

Essay questions often include a scenario. To make sure you achieve the highest marks, your answer should be written in the context of the scenario.

EXAM TIP 

The quality of the written answer, using technical language, is just as important as the number of different points covered, when answering essay questions.

2 Outline **two** features of open-source software. **[4]**

EXAM TIP 

In preparation for your exam, you should be able to describe how technology brings benefits, and how technology can bring problems.

3 A business has five computers (laptops and desktops) used by the whole office. They would like a license for a suite of software to use on all of these computers to include at least:

- word processing
- spreadsheet
- database.

They would like the same software on all the machines, to be sure of compatibility.

You have been asked to recommend to them a type of software license for this scenario.

State the type of software license you would recommend for this scenario **and** identify **two** drawbacks and **two** benefits for using this type of license. **[6]**

EXAM TIP

This scenario question can be correct with either of the types of software licence being chosen provided the benefits and drawbacks match the type of license **and** the scenario. This is not true of all questions of this type, so make sure you thoroughly read the scenario before answering.

15 Computational thinking

Problem recognition

Computational thinking is a method of problem solving. It means using the rules of logic and maths to solve a problem. Not all problems can be solved by computational thinking.

Problem recognition means setting out the problem you need to solve. Setting out the problem is the first step to finding a solution.

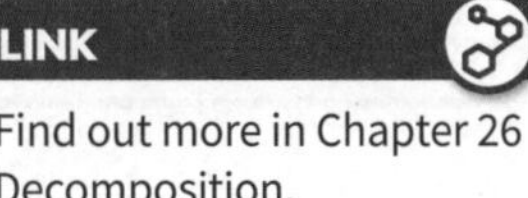

Find out more in Chapter 26 Decomposition.

Complex problems have lots of parts and details. Simple problems are smaller with fewer details. It is easier to solve simple problems than complex problems.

Abstraction

Abstraction means simplifying a problem to include only the facts that are necessary to solve it.

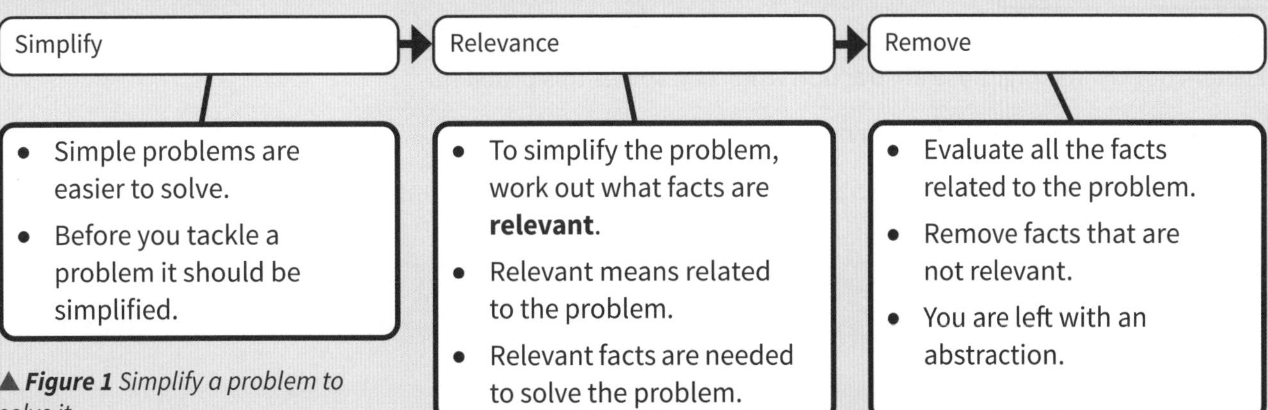

Simplify
Relevance
Remove
• Simple problems are easier to solve.
• Before you tackle a problem it should be simplified.
• To simplify the problem, work out what facts are **relevant**.
• Relevant means related to the problem.
• Relevant facts are needed to solve the problem.
• Evaluate all the facts related to the problem.
• Remove facts that are not relevant.
• You are left with an abstraction.

▲ ***Figure 1*** *Simplify a problem to solve it*

Which facts you remove depends on the problem. Different problems need different facts.

IPO model (input, processing, output)

You can use an **IPO** (**input, processing, output**) **model** to describe a problem.

LINK

Find out more in Chapter 20 Inputs and outputs.

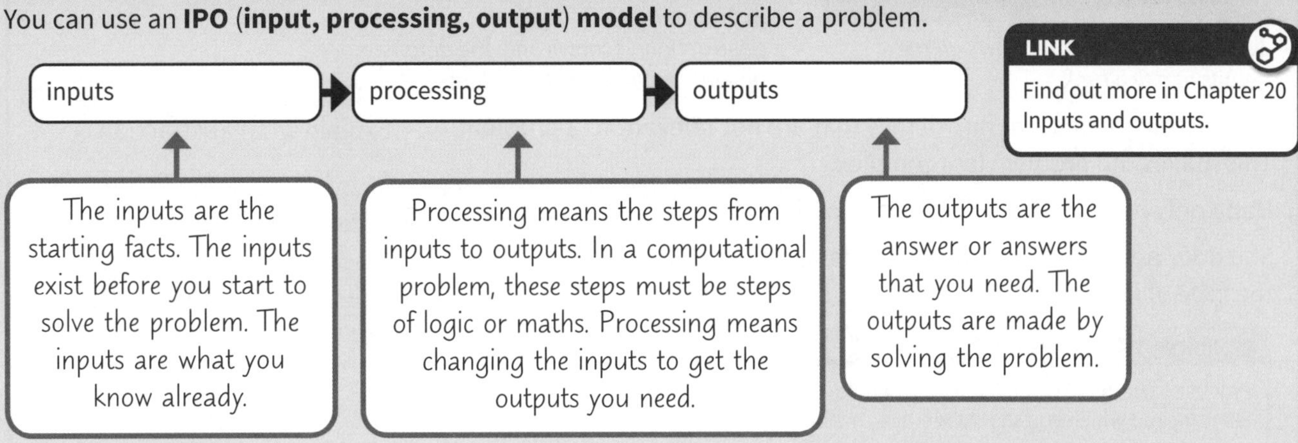

inputs
processing
outputs
The inputs are the starting facts. The inputs exist before you start to solve the problem. The inputs are what you know already.
Processing means the steps from inputs to outputs. In a computational problem, these steps must be steps of logic or maths. Processing means changing the inputs to get the outputs you need.
The outputs are the answer or answers that you need. The outputs are made by solving the problem.

▲ ***Figure 2*** *The IPO model*

Knowledge

15 Computational thinking

Algorithms

In a computational problem, there are logical or mathematical steps that turn inputs into outputs.

An **algorithm** sets out the logical or mathematical steps to solve a problem.

LINK

Find out more in Chapter 16 Writing algorithms.

A good algorithm should be...

- accurate; it solves the problem
- repeatable; you can use the algorithm with different inputs and it always gives you the right answer
- understandable; each step should be clearly set out so anyone can understand it

Worked example 1

Hana has a fish tank in her room. She needs to find the volume of the fish tank. Explain how Hana might use abstraction when she solves this problem.

In this example, you need to use abstraction.

Abstraction means removing details that are not relevant. Focus on what details are relevant to the problem.

Relevant facts include the height, width, and length of the tank.

Irrelevant facts include the type of fish in the tank.

▲ ***Figure 3*** *This image shows all the details of a fish tank.*

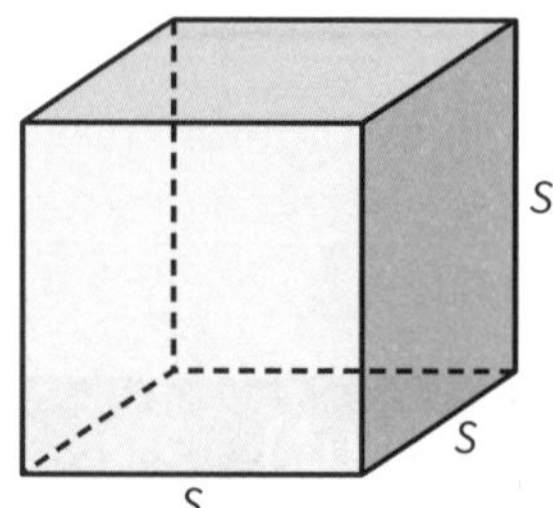

▲ ***Figure 4*** *This image is an abstraction; it shows only the details needed to calculate the volume.*

Abstraction means ignoring details that are not relevant to a problem. This makes the problem less complex. — Explain what abstraction is.

Hana only needs to consider the size of the fish tank. — Set out which details are relevant.

She does not need to include other details such as the type of fish in the tank. — Give an example of details that are not relevant.

REVISION TIP

Practise identifying what details you should leave in, and which you should remove.

Algorithms

Worked example 2

Hana has a fish tank in his room. She needs to find the volume of the fish tank.
Create an IPO model of the problem.

The question will include everything you need to find inputs, processes, and outputs.

Inputs: the length, height, and width of the tank

The inputs are facts relevant to the problem. Think about the facts that are available. Use abstraction to leave out facts that are not relevant.

Processes: length × width × height = volume

Processes are the calculations or logical steps that will turn inputs into outputs.

Outputs: the volume of the tank

The outputs are the results that you need. Reading the question carefully should tell you the output that is needed.

Set the three items out in the order inputs, processes, outputs.

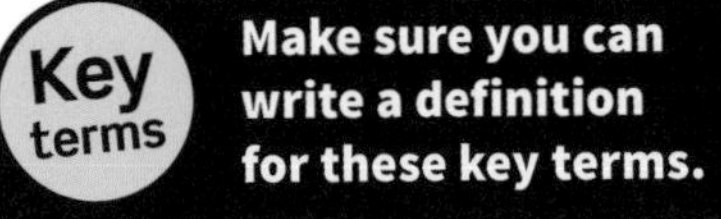
Key terms
Make sure you can write a definition for these key terms.

abstraction algorithm input IPO (input, processing, output) model output processing relevant

Retrieval

Learn the answers to the questions below, then cover the answers column with a piece of paper and write down as many answers as you can. Check and repeat.

	Questions	Answers
1	What are the features of a problem that can be solved by computational methods?	a problem that can be solved by computational methods can be solved using logic or maths
2	What is the difference between a complex problem and a simple problem?	complex problems have lots of parts and details; simple problems are smaller with fewer details; it is easier to solve simple problems
3	When thinking about a problem, some details are relevant. What does relevant mean?	relevant means necessary for solving the problem
4	Explain the difference between an abstraction and a complete description of a problem.	an abstraction is a simplified description that only includes relevant details; a complete description includes details not relevant to solving the problem
5	How can you create an abstraction?	think about what details are relevant to the problem; leave out all other details
6	What are the parts of an IPO model?	inputs, processing, and outputs
7	What are the inputs to a problem?	inputs are the relevant facts that are available before you start to solve the problem
8	What are the outputs to a problem?	outputs are the results that you need; when you have solved the problem, you will have the outputs
9	In a computational problem, how are inputs linked to outputs?	in a computational problem you can get from the inputs to the outputs using logical or mathematical steps
10	What is an algorithm?	an algorithm sets out the logical or mathematical steps to solve a problem, by turning inputs into outputs

Put paper here

Previous questions

Now go back and use the questions below to check your knowledge from previous chapters.

	Previous questions	Answers
1	What are the advantages and disadvantages of ASCII compared to Unicode?	ASCII uses less storage space for each character, but it has a more restricted character set than Unicode
2	Define a user interface.	the user interface allows the user to work with the computer sending and receiving information
3	What is a peripheral device? Give two typical functions of peripheral devices.	a peripheral device is a device attached to the computer processor (e.g. input and output devices)
4	What happens at the fetch stage of the fetch–execute cycle?	electronic instructions and data travel from the memory unit to the control unit

Put paper here

Exam-style questions

A rectangular shaped room is to be fitted with a new carpet. The room measures 10 × 5 metres. The carpet will be made from wool, and it is 1 centimetre thick. The carpet costs £35 per square metre. The price of the carpet to be fitted will be calculated.

1 Describe what is meant by abstraction. **[2]**

2 Identify the relevant facts from the given scenario after abstraction has been applied. **[2]**

3 State the inputs, processes, and outputs from the given scenario. **[3]**

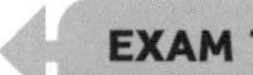

EXAM TIP

For an IPO model, if no row heading is given, arrange your answer as input, process, output.

Knowledge

16 Writing algorithms

Why write an algorithm?

An **algorithm** sets out the steps to solve a problem. You can follow the algorithm as you solve the problem. Or you can use the algorithm to guide you as you write a computer program.

Sometimes it is useful to write down an algorithm because it helps you to:

- remember the algorithm to use another time
- tell other people about the algorithm
- check, fix, or improve the algorithm.

There are four ways to write an algorithm:

1. a high level programming language
2. **pseudocode**
3. Exam Reference Language
4. a **flowchart**.

Contents of an algorithm

An algorithm must set out the contents of the IPO model in full detail and show:

Inputs: the values that are input into the algorithm and in what order.

Processing: how values are changed using logical or mathematical processes; what processes are used and in what order.

Outputs: the values that are output by the algorithm and when this happens.

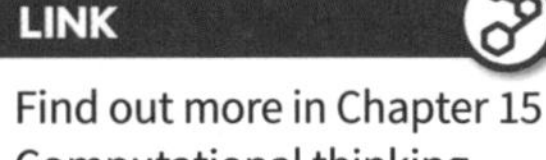

Find out more in Chapter 15 Computational thinking.

High level languages

You can write an algorithm in a programming language. Examples include Python or Java. Not every programmer will know every programming language. That means lots of programmers will not understand your algorithm.

Find out more in Chapter 17 Programming languages.

Pseudocode

Programmers often write algorithms in pseudocode. 'Pseudo' means 'pretend'. Pseudocode is pretend program code. Pseudocode can be shared and understood by programmers who know different programming languages.

Pseudocode does not have strict rules. Programmers just use their common sense. The idea is to write code in a way that other programmers can understand.

Many websites show useful algorithms. The algorithms are often written in pseudocode. Different forms of pseudocode are used.

REVISION TIP 

Some exam questions include a sample of program code. The sample will be written using exam reference language.

Exam Reference Language

The OCR Computer Science exam includes questions about algorithms and program code. Sometimes a question includes a sample of code.

These samples will be written in a special form of pseudocode called OCR Exam Reference Language (ERL).

Exam Reference Language is different from typical pseudocode. It has strict rules. That means the code will be easy for you to read and understand. It is reliable and consistent.

```
function square(number)
    new = number ** 2
    return new
endfunction
```

▲ ***Figure 1** An example of exam reference language*

LINK 

Find out more in Appendix A Exam Reference Language.

REVISION TIP 

All the examples of code in this book are written using OCR Exam Reference Language.

Knowledge

16 Writing algorithms

Flowcharts

Another way to write an algorithm is using a flowchart. Flowcharts are diagrams that show the structure of an algorithm. They are made of boxes joined by arrows. The arrows point down the page.

LINK

Find out more in Chapter 21 Selection structure.

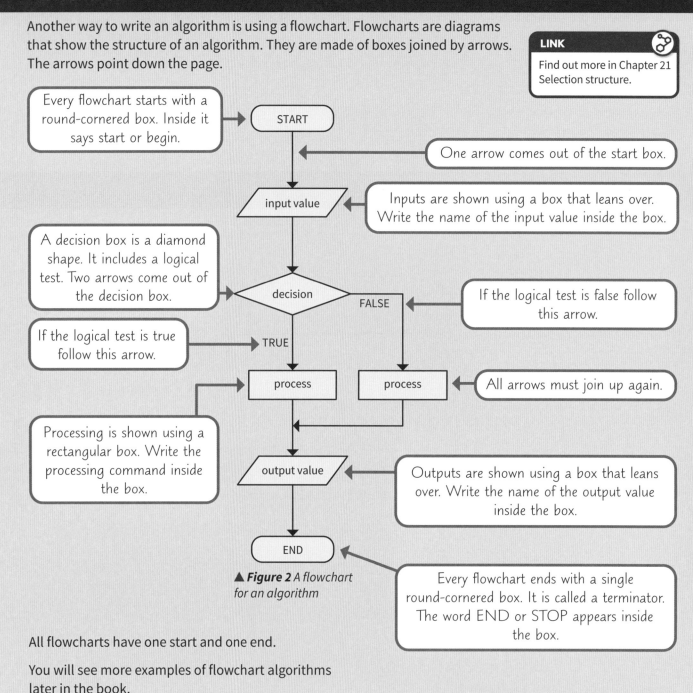

Every flowchart starts with a round-cornered box. Inside it says start or begin.

START

One arrow comes out of the start box.

input value

Inputs are shown using a box that leans over. Write the name of the input value inside the box.

A decision box is a diamond shape. It includes a logical test. Two arrows come out of the decision box.

decision

FALSE

If the logical test is false follow this arrow.

If the logical test is true follow this arrow.

TRUE

process

process

All arrows must join up again.

Processing is shown using a rectangular box. Write the processing command inside the box.

output value

Outputs are shown using a box that leans over. Write the name of the output value inside the box.

END

Every flowchart ends with a single round-cornered box. It is called a terminator. The word END or STOP appears inside the box.

▲ ***Figure 2*** *A flowchart for an algorithm*

All flowcharts have one start and one end.

You will see more examples of flowchart algorithms later in the book.

Compare ways of writing algorithms

Writing algorithms using ...	Advantages	Disadvantages
High level language	Makes a working program you can use right away.	Will not be understood by all programmers.
Pseudocode	You can share code with programmers in all languages.	The code does not work as a program on a computer.
Exam Reference Language	Has standard consistent rules which you can learn.	Like pseudocode it does not m ake a program that works.
Flowchart	Easy to read and understand, especially if you are a visual thinker.	Even quite a short algorithm takes up a lot of space.

Make sure you can write a definition for these key terms.

algorithm flowchart pseudocode

Retrieval

Learn the answers to the questions below, then cover the answers column with a piece of paper and write down as many answers as you can. Check and repeat.

	Questions	Answers
1	Why might you want to write down an algorithm?	to remember it for another time; to tell other people about it; to check, fix, or improve it
2	What are the ways you might write out an algorithm?	algorithms can be written in pseudocode, a high level language, or using a flowchart
3	What are the rules of the pseudocode language?	pseudocode does not have strict rules; programmers use common sense to write text that can be read by other programmers
4	What is the advantage of writing an algorithm using a flowchart instead of pseudocode?	a flowchart algorithm may be easier to understand, especially if you are a visual thinker
5	Draw or describe the box that starts a flowchart. How many arrows come out of this box?	a box with rounded corners; one arrow comes out START
6	Draw or describe the box used for input or output values in a flowchart algorithm. What goes inside the box?	a leaning-over box, with the input or output input value
7	Draw or describe a decision box. What is inside the box? Show how arrows come out of the box.	a diamond-shaped box with a logical decision in it; arrows come out to the right and down; labelled true and false decision TRUE FALSE
8	Explain why a flowchart might have more than one arrow going down the page but always ends with a single arrow.	the arrows must join up again before the end of the flowchart
9	How is a process shown in a flowchart? Draw or describe the box.	a rectangular box with the process in it process
10	Draw or describe the box that you will always find at the bottom of a flowchart.	a box with round corners and END or STOP END

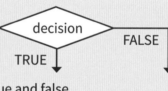

Put paper here

Previous questions

Now go back and use the questions below to check your knowledge from previous chapters.

	Previous questions	Answers
1	When thinking about a problem, some details are relevant. What does relevant mean?	relevant means necessary for solving the problem
2	Explain the difference between an abstraction and a complete description of a problem.	an abstraction is a simplified description that only includes relevant details; a complete description includes details not relevant to solving the problem
3	What is copyright?	the right to decide who can use or copy creative content that you made

Put paper here

Exam-style questions

1 An algorithm can be written using many techniques, including pseudocode, flowcharts, and high level languages.

Outline **one** reason to write an algorithm using pseudocode. **[2]**

2 Complete the table by drawing the flowchart symbol that matches each symbol name.

EXAM TIP

Do not use a flowchart to show your answer unless the question clearly tells you to do so.

Symbol name	Flowchart symbol
Input/Output	
Decision	
Sub-program	

[3]

3 State **one** advantage and **one** disadvantage of writing an algorithm using Java rather than the OCR Exam Reference Language. **[2]**

EXAM TIP

Some questions ask you to write program code. You can write the code using either OCR Exam Reference Language or a high level programming language you have studied.

Knowledge

17 Programming languages

Write a program

There are many programming languages. These include Python, Java, and C++.

You can write a program using a programming language. A program is a series of commands. When you run the program, the computer will carry out the commands. The program controls what the computer does.

Write a program	Translate	Run the program
• A programmer writes a series of commands using a programming language.	• The computer converts the program into computer-readable commands.	• The computer carries out the commands. • The program controls what the computer does.

▲ ***Figure 1*** *What happens when you write and run a program*

REVISION TIP 

The best way to learn about programming is to practice writing programs in the programming language of your choice.

LINK 

Find out more in Chapter 4 The processor.

Use an IDE

Most programming languages are text-based. That means the commands are written using ordinary keyboard characters. You can write a program using any software that makes plain text files.

There is software designed especially for writing programs. This software is called an **integrated development environment** (**IDE**). Most programmers use an IDE when they write programs.

An IDE has many features that help programmers.

- **Editing tools:** Text editing features like delete, copy, replace. This makes it quick and easy to type the program code.
- **Error diagnostics:** If you make an error the IDE will show you an error message. This will tell you where the error is, and what type of error it is.
- **Translator**: Turns your commands into signals the computer can understand.
- **Run-time environment**: Shows the results of the program.

REVISION TIP 

Learn the names of all key IDE features, even if the IDE you are used to does not include them.

REVISION TIP 

Think of error diagnostics in the same way a doctor diagnoses an illness. They find out and tell you what is wrong.

LINK 

Find out more in Chapter 23 Coding errors.

Use an IDE

An IDE includes error **diagnostics**. That means the IDE spots errors in your code. It tells you what is wrong. An IDE cannot spot every error in your code. It can only spot certain types of error, such as misspelt command words.

```
File  Edit  Format  Run  Options  Window  Help
total = (   Run Module        F5
for i in r  Run... Customized Shift+F5
            Check Module      Alt+X
            Python Shell
    num = input("enter a number: ")
    num = int(num)
    total = total + num
print(total)
```

▲ ***Figure 2** An IDE lets you write and run program code*

Translator

The computer cannot understand program code. The computer can only understand commands in a language called machine code. These commands are made of binary numbers. It is difficult for a human programmer to write machine code.

A file made of machine code is called an executable file. You can 'run' the file and the computer will carry out the commands. Most of the apps on your computer or phone are executable files.

Before the computer can run the program, all the commands must be turned into machine code. This is called translation. The software that does it is called a **translator**. All IDEs include a translator.

There are two types of translator: a **compiler** and an **interpreter**. They work in different ways.

REVISION TIP 

Try more than one programming language to get experience with different types of translator.

	Compiler	Interpreter
How it works	Reads the whole program Turns the whole program into machine code Saves the machine code as a new file	Reads one command at a time Makes the computer carry out that command Does not save any new code
Benefits	Once the program is compiled you don't have to compile it again You end up with a machine code file that you can give or sell to others	A quick way to try out new commands and see the results instantly
Drawbacks	You don't see the results until you run the machine code file Every time you make a change to the program you have to make a new machine code file	Every time you want to run the program you have to translate it again You have no machine code file at the end to sell
Use for...	Making programs to sell	Learning and exploring programming

▲ ***Figure 3** The differences between a compiler and an interpreter*

17 Programming languages

Run-time environment

When the program has been translated it can be run. The outputs of the program appear in the **run-time environment**. For example, when you are using the Python IDE, the run-time environment is the Python shell.

```
enter a number: 10
enter a number: 4
enter a number: b
Traceback (most recent call last):
  File "C:/Users/Alison/Documents/2022 work organiser/.
t drafts/2aii sample.py", line 4, in <module>
    num = int(num)
ValueError: invalid literal for int() with base 10: 'b'
```

▲ ***Figure 4*** *The run-time environment showing an error message*

The run-time environment:

- lets the user input values.
- shows the outputs of the program
- shows any run-time errors.

High level and low level languages

Most programming languages are **high level languages**. That means they are made to be easy for the human programmer. High level languages suit the way humans work. Python, Java, and C++ are high level languages.

Some programming languages are **low level languages**. They are not so easy to use. They match the way computers work. Machine code and assembly language are low level languages.

High level languages	Low level languages
Good for human programmers Used for almost all complex software	Match the way the computer works Good for small programs that need close control over the computer's hardware
Examples: apps, games	Examples: utilities, device drivers, virus checkers

▲ ***Figure 5*** *The differences between high level and low level languages*

LINK

Find out more in Chapter 6 Operating systems.

Key terms
Make sure you can write a definition for these key terms.

compiler diagnostic high level language integrated development environment (IDE) interpreter low level language run-time environment translator

Retrieval

Learn the answers to the questions below, then cover the answers column with a piece of paper and write down as many answers as you can. Check and repeat.

	Questions	Answers
1	What is an IDE?	IDE is short for integrated development environment; this is software designed for writing programs
2	What are the key features of an IDE?	editing tools, error diagnostics, a translator, and a run-time environment
3	How do error diagnostics help a programmer to write code?	error diagnostics find errors and display an error message to say where and what type of error it
4	What is a translator? Why do programmers need to use a translator?	the computer can only understand commands in machine code; a translator turns the commands of a programming language into machine code
5	What are the two types of translator?	the two types of translator are a compiler and an interpreter
6	What does a compiler do?	a compiler reads the whole program and turns it into machine code, making a new file
7	What are the advantages and disadvantages of a compiler?	advantage, you only have to translate once; then you have an executable file to use or sell; disadvantage, each time you make a change you have to create a run a new file of machine code
8	What does an interpreter do?	an interpreter reads one command at a time and makes the computer carry out that command; it does not save any new code
9	What are the advantages and disadvantages of an interpreter?	advantage: you can quickly change a program and see the effects; disadvantages: you need to translate the program every time you run it, and you don't have an executable file to sell or use
10	What is the purpose of the run-time environment?	the run-time environment shows the outputs of the program; it is also where the user provides input, and error messages are displayed
11	Explain the difference between high level and low level languages	high level languages suit the way humans work. They are the easiest to use. Low level languages are not so easy. They match the way computers work

Put paper here

Previous questions

Now go back and use the questions below to check your knowledge from previous chapters.

	Previous questions	Answers
1	How can you create an abstraction?	think about what details are relevant to the problem; leave out all other details
2	What are the parts of an IPO model?	inputs, processing, and outputs
3	What are the ways you might write out an algorithm?	algorithms can be written in pseudocode, a high level language, or using a flowchart

Put paper here

Practice

Exam-style questions

1 Identify **two** characteristics of using a compiler to translate program code into machine readable code. **[2]**

> **EXAM TIP**
> Make sure you know the differences between compilers and interpreters and when it would be best to use each type.

2 Identify **two** benefits and **two** drawbacks of using an interpreter to translate program code into machine readable code. **[2]**

3 Complete the table by writing the missing name or description for each integrated development environment (IDE) tool.

> **EXAM TIP**
> Make sure to note the tools available in the IDE when you are writing your programs.

IDE tool	Description
Editors	
	Identifies errors with error messages and locations of errors
Run-time environment	
Translators	

[4]

4 A programmer has decided to write their program using a high level language.

Explain why a programmer would find a high level language easier to use for writing programs than a low level language. **[3]**

18 Values and variables

Expressions

The basic structure of a program is shown by the IPO model. Values are input, then changed by processing, and the new values are output.

In programming languages, values are represented using expressions. The simplest form of expression just shows the value. This type of expression is called a 'literal' or 'simple' expression. Examples of literal expressions include:

- 34
- 12.7
- 'Hello'.

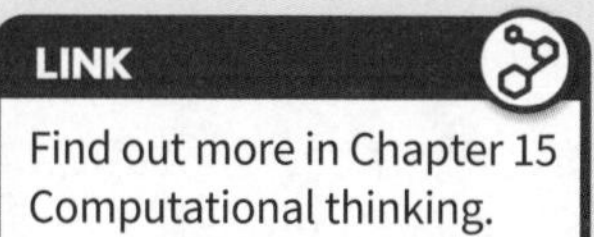

LINK

Find out more in Chapter 15 Computational thinking.

You can evaluate a literal expression just by looking at it. Evaluating an expression means finding its value.

Data types

Every expression has a **data type**.

Name of data type	Meaning of data type	Examples	Notes
Integer	Whole number with no decimal point	1 −6 453000	Numbers can be negative (minus numbers). Never include a comma in the number.
Real (also called float)	Number with a decimal point in it	1.2 −6.5 12.0	The value after the decimal point can be 0.
Boolean	Logical true or false	True False	The words do not have quote marks round them.
Character	A single text character in quote marks	'a' '?' '3'	Characters do not have to be letters of the alphabet – any character you can type can be used.
String	A series of text characters in quote marks	'hello again' ":{3$" '306'	Quote marks can be 'single' or "double". Strings can hold a single character, or more than one character.

▲ ***Figure 1*** *Data types*

You can only carry out calculations with numerical values. The only numerical data types are integer and real. You cannot do calculations with Boolean, string, or character values.

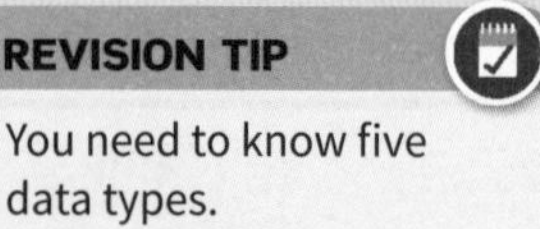

REVISION TIP

You need to know five data types.

The Boolean data type is named after George Boole, a mathematician who invented the rules of modern logic.

18 Values and variables

Variables

Most programs get and make new values. It is a good idea to save the values to use later in the program. To save a value, you must send it to the computer's memory (or RAM). The value will be stored in a memory location.

A memory location where values are stored is called a **variable**. That's because the value stored there can vary. It can change while the program is running.

Every memory location has an address. The address is a binary number. A memory address is hard for a programmer to remember and type, so variables are given names. The name is called the identifier of the variable.

LINK
Find out more in Chapter 5 Electronic memory.

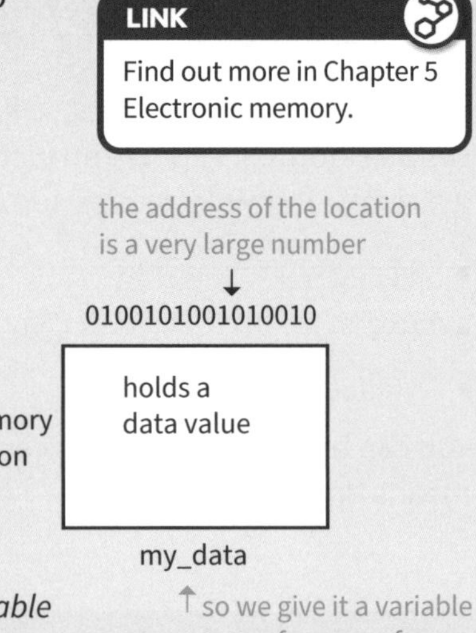

▶ ***Figure 2*** *Variable address and name*

Assign a value to a variable

A variable is a named memory location. To store a value in that memory location you need to **assign** a value to the variable. This is done with the equals sign. The command has this structure.

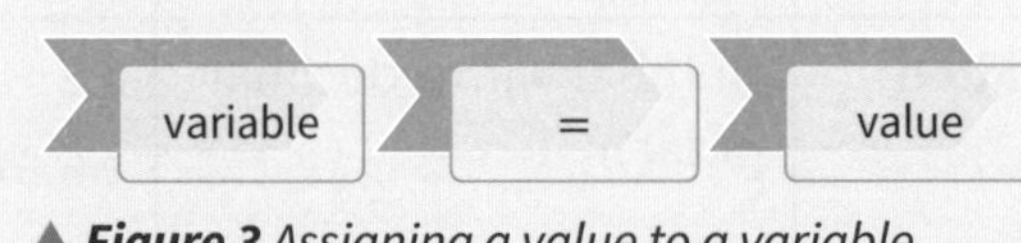

▲ ***Figure 3*** *Assigning a value to a variable*

For example, the command

```
age = 16
```

assigns the value 16 to a variable called age.

Good identifiers

There are some rules for good variable names. The rules can vary between programming languages.

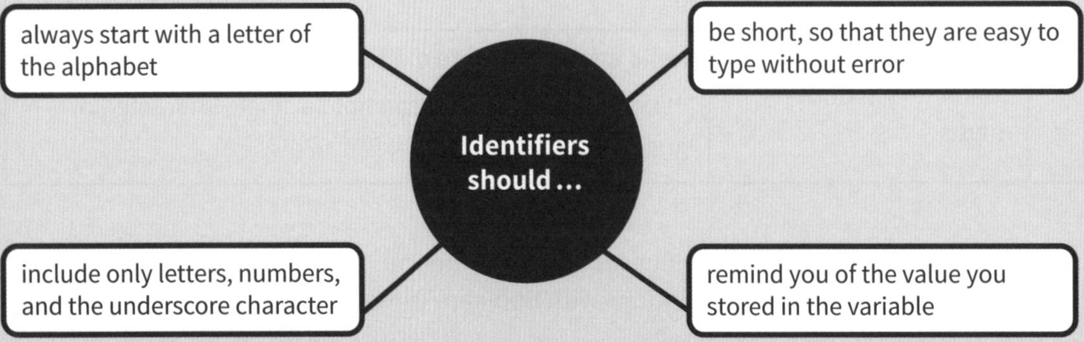

Identifiers should ...
always start with a letter of the alphabet
be short, so that they are easy to type without error
include only letters, numbers, and the underscore character
remind you of the value you stored in the variable

Using good identifiers makes your program more readable.

String values have quotation marks around them. Identifiers such as variable names do not have quotation marks.

Change the value of a variable

The value of a variable can change. Simply assign a new value to the variable. The new value will overwrite the old value.

For example, the command

```
age = 25
```

will put the new value 25 into the variable age. The old value is lost.

Constants

Sometimes you want to store a value that will not change while the program is running. To do this, make the variable into a **constant**. The key word 'const' will do this.

For example, the command

```
const age = 19
```

will store the value 19 with the identifier age. The value of age is then fixed. It cannot be overwritten. If you try to change it, there will be a program error.

Only some languages allow you to make constants.

How to select the right data type

1. If the value is in quote marks, choose one of the text data types:
   - If the length is 1, use a character or string.
   - For any other length, use a string.
2. If the value is a number, choose one of the numerical data types:
   - If there is no decimal point, use an integer.
   - If there is a decimal point, use a real or float.
3. The only other valid data type is Boolean. The allowed values are True and False.

Key terms
Make sure you can write a definition for these key terms.

assign Boolean character constant data type float integer real string variable

Retrieval

Learn the answers to the questions below, then cover the answers column with a piece of paper and write down as many answers as you can. Check and repeat.

	Questions	Answers
1	What are the numerical data types?	the numerical data types are integer and real (or float)
2	What is the difference between the numerical data types?	integers are whole numbers; reals can include a decimal point
3	What data types can be used to store text values? What is the difference between them?	text values can be stored using the character and string data types; a character can store a single character only; a string can store any number of characters
4	What values can be held by an expression of the Boolean data type?	a Boolean expression can have the value True or False
5	What is a variable?	a variable is a named location in the computer's memory
6	What is the identifier of a variable?	the identifier is the name of the variable
7	How do you store a value in a variable? What is this called?	use the command variable = value; this is called assignment (or assigning a value)
8	How do you change the value stored in a variable? What happens to the old value?	a variable can be assigned a new value, by using a new assignment command; the new value will overwrite the old value; the old value is lost
9	How do you store a value as a constant?	put the command word 'const' in front of the assignment statement
10	What is the difference between a variable and a constant?	the original value assigned to a constant cannot be changed or overwritten while the program is running

Put paper here

Previous questions

Now go back and use the questions below to check your knowledge from previous chapters.

	Previous questions	Answers
1	What is an algorithm?	an algorithm sets out the logical or mathematical steps to solve a problem, by turning inputs into outputs
2	What is a translator? Why do programmers need to use a translator?	the computer can only understand commands if they are in machine code; a translator turns the commands of a programming language into machine code
3	What are the two types of translator?	the two types of translator are a compiler and an interpreter
4	What is the purpose of the run-time environment?	the run-time environment shows the outputs of the program; it is also where the user provides input, and error messages are displayed
5	Draw or describe the box that starts a flowchart. How many arrows come out of this box?	a box with rounded corners; one arrow comes out of the box START

Put paper here

Exam-style questions

1 Complete the table by writing a description and giving an example of sample data for each of the data types.

Data type	Description	Sample data
Boolean		
Character		
Integer		

[6]

2 A variable needs to be assigned the value "`Peter`" **and** a constant needs to be assigned the value 2025.

Write pseudocode to assign the given values to a variable and a constant, using appropriate identifiers. **[2]**

EXAM TIP

This question asks for pseudocode, so it is best to answer using the OCR Exam Reference Language.

3 Identify **two** features **or** rules that should be applied when naming variables. **[2]**

EXAM TIP 

A good naming convention makes it easier to understand and maintain a program.

Knowledge

19 Operators

Making values

Every computer program includes processing. Processing changes values. Operators are symbols that change values. For example, the + operator adds two number values to give a new number.

There are three important groups of operator:

- **arithmetic operators**
- **comparison** (or relational) **operators**
- **Boolean operators**.

Arithmetic as in 'arithmetic operator' is pronounced 'arith-MET-ic'.

Using an operator creates a new expression. Every expression holds a value. A program command can output that value or assign the value to a variable.

The action performed by an operator is called an operation.

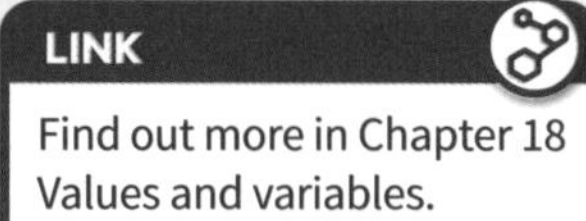
LINK
Find out more in Chapter 18 Values and variables.

Arithmetic operators

Arithmetic operators carry out numerical operations. They change number values.

In Exam Reference Language the operators are written using these symbols.

The normal division operator is /.

This operator gives a result with a decimal point in it. The result of the calculation is the real (or float) data type.

For example, the result of 7 / 2 is 3.5.

Raising to the power is the operation shown in maths like this:

2^4

That expression means '2 to the power 4' or 2 × 2 × 2 × 2. This expression has the value 16.

In Exam Reference Language the same expression would be written as:

2**4

Operator	What it does
+	Addition
–	Subtraction
*	Multiplication
/	Division
^	Exponentiation (to the power)

▲ ***Figure 1*** *Arithmetic operators*

Other types of division

There are two more arithmetic operators that are used for division. They are used for integer division. Integer division means division with remainders.

The operators are DIV and MOD.

Operator	Description	What it means
DIV	**Quotient**	Integer division: Divide one number by another and show the whole number part of the result.
MOD	**Modulus**	Remainder: Divide one number by another and show the remainder only.

▲ ***Figure 2*** *Integer division operators*

For example, the result of 7 divided by 2 is 3 remainder 1 when you use integer division.

The quotient is 3. So the result of 7 DIV 2 is 3.

The remainder is 1. So the result of 7 MOD 2 is 1.

Arithmetic operators and data types

Arithmetic operators can only be used with numerical data. That means the integer and real data types. If you use arithmetic operators with other types of data you will get a program error.

The output of an arithmetic expression is always a numerical data type. The output will be integer or real.

- If an expression has two integers, such as 3 + 5, then the result is an integer.
- If an expression includes at least one real data type, such as 3 + 5.1 then the result is a real.
- The result of the division operator / is always a real.
- The result of the integer division operators DIV or MOD is always an integer.

REVISION TIP

Practice using operators by writing programs in a high level language.

19 Operators

Comparison operators

Comparison operators are used to compare two values. They may also be called relational operators.

Key comparison operators are shown in **Figure 3**.

Operator	Comparison
= =	Equal to
! =	Not equal to
<	Less than
< =	Less than or equal to
>	Greater than
> =	Greater than or equal to

◀ ***Figure 3*** *Comparison operators*

A comparison represents the relationship between the two values. The result of a comparison is either True or False.

For example, the expression 7 < 3 is False, because 7 is not smaller than 3.

The result of a comparison operator is always a Boolean value. An expression that results in a Boolean value is called a **Boolean expression**.

Boolean operators

Boolean expressions can have the value True or False.

Boolean operators are used with Boolean expressions. They make a larger Boolean expression.

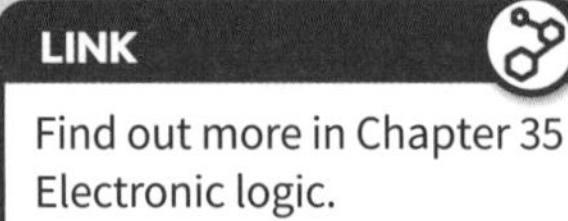

Find out more in Chapter 35 Electronic logic.

Operator	What it does	What is the value of the new expression
AND	Joins two Boolean expressions.	The expression is True if both the original expressions are True.
OR	Joins two Boolean expressions.	The expression is True if one or both of the original expressions is True.
NOT	Reverses the value of a Boolean expression.	If the original expression is True, the new expression is False. If the original expression is False, the new expression is True.

▲ ***Figure 4*** *Boolean operators*

For example, the expression NOT(7 < 3) is True because the expression (7 < 3) is False and NOT reverses the truth value.

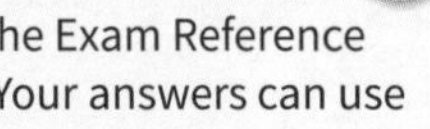

REVISION TIP

The questions in the exam will always use the Exam Reference Language operators shown in this section. Your answers can use operators from any high level language that you know.

Overview

Figure 5 summarises the rules about operators and data types.

Type of operator	Used with ...	Makes ...
Arithmetic	Numerical values	A numerical expression
Comparison	Any two expressions or values	A Boolean expression
Boolean	Boolean expressions	A larger Boolean expression

▲ ***Figure 5*** *Summary of operators and data types*

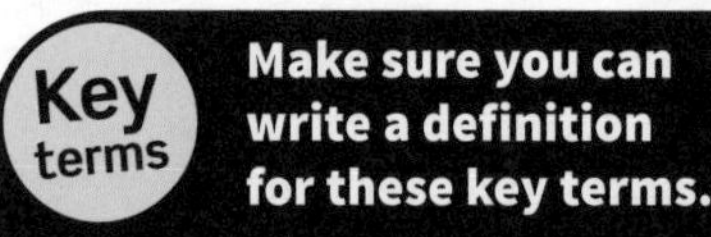

Make sure you can write a definition for these key terms.

arithmetic operator   Boolean expression   Boolean operator   comparison operator   modulus   quotient

Retrieval

Learn the answers to the questions below, then cover the answers column with a piece of paper and write down as many answers as you can. Check and repeat.

	Questions	Answers
1	What are the three types of operator?	arithmetic, comparison, and Boolean.
2	What is exponentiation?	exponentiation means raising one number to the power of another; that means multiplying the first number by itself several times; the number of times to do this is shown by the second number
3	What is integer division?	integer division means dividing one number by another and giving the result as a whole value (the quotient) plus a remainder (the modulus)
4	What two operators are used for integer division? What are the results of these operators?	the two operators used for integer division are DIV and MOD; DIV gives the quotient, and MOD gives the modulus or remainder
5	What is the data type of an expression made using the division operator / ?	expressions made using the division operator are real (or float) data type
6	What is the data type of an expression made using a comparison operator?	an expression made using a comparison operator is the Boolean data type
7	How do you work out the result of an expression that uses the comparison operator == ?	see if the two values being compared are equal or different in value; if they are equal the result is True; if they are different the result is False
8	What is the meaning of the comparison operator !=?	the comparison operator != means 'not equal to'; the expression is True if the values being compared are not equal
9	What are the three Boolean operators?	the three Boolean operators are AND, OR, NOT
10	What is the result of the NOT operator?	the NOT operator reverses the value of a Boolean expression

Put paper here

Previous questions

Now go back and use the questions below to check your knowledge from previous chapters.

	Previous questions	Answers
1	What is a variable?	a variable is a named location in the computer's memory
2	How do you store a value in a variable? What is this called?	use the command variable = value; this is called assignment (or assigning a value)
3	What is an IDE?	IDE is short for integrated development environment; this is software designed for writing programs
4	How do error diagnostics help a programmer to write code?	error diagnostics find errors and display an error message to say where the error is and what type of error it is
5	How do you store a value as a constant?	put the command word 'const' in front of the assignment statement

Put paper here

Exam-style questions

1 State the purpose of each of the arithmetic operators in the table.

Operator	Purpose
+	
*	
MOD	

[3]

2 Write pseudocode to:

- calculate the value of the number held in the variable `store` raised to the power of the number held in the variable `power`
- assign this new value to the variable `answer`. **[2]**

EXAM TIP

Algorithm questions often give a list of the requirements for the algorithm.

EXAM TIP

If the question asks for pseudocode, it is best to answer using the OCR Exam Reference Language.

3 State **two** common Boolean operators. **[2]**

EXAM TIP

'State' questions require answers that can usually be single words or very short expressions.

Knowledge

20 Inputs and outputs

The structure of an algorithm

All algorithms follow a typical structure.

Inputs: starting values go into the algorithm. → **Processing**: the inputs are changed to make new values, for example by operators. → **Outputs**: the new values are displayed.

LINK 

Find out more in Chapter 19 Operators.

REVISION TIP 

Practise drawing simple diagrams to help you remember the structure.

Inputs

Most programs begin with inputs. Inputs are values entered by the user. In a text-based programming language the inputs are text characters. The inputs are typed by the user with the keyboard.

In Exam Reference Language the command to get input is:

```
input("prompt")
```

Instead of the word *prompt* write some prompt text. The prompt text is a message to the user. It tells the user what value they have to input.

```
input("enter your age:")
```

The value input by the user should be assigned to a variable. So the full input command is:

```
variable = input("prompt")
```

Instead of the word *variable*, give the identifier of the variable where the value will be stored.

LINK 

Find out more in Chapter 28 Safe and readable programs.

```
age = input("enter your age:")
```

In a typical text-based program, the inputs are text characters typed in by the user. In many languages, input values are stored using the string data type. Even if the user inputs digits, they are stored as a string.

LINK 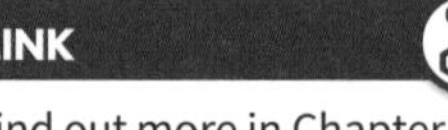

Find out more in Chapter 18 Values and variables.

Outputs

A program can output the value of any expression.

In Exam Reference Language the command to produce output is:

```
print()
```

You can put any expression inside the brackets. The output expression can be any data type. The computer will evaluate that expression (find out its value). It will display the value.

```
print(age)
```

There can be more than one expression inside the brackets. Separate the expressions with commas. The computer will output all the values on the same line.

Change data type (casting)

In many languages, inputs are stored as the string data type. Arithmetic operators can only work with numerical data types. That means you cannot use arithmetic operators with input values.

You need to convert the input variable to a numerical data type. Changing the data type of a variable is called **casting**.

In Exam Reference Language there are five functions to cast a variable.

Function name	What it does
`int()`	Convert the variable to integer data type.
`real()` `float()`	Convert the variable to real or float data type.
`string()`	Convert the variable to string data type.
`boolean()`	Convert the variable to Boolean data type.

▲ ***Figure 1*** *The functions to cast a variable*

The name of the variable to be cast goes inside the brackets. A new value is created by the function. The new value should be assigned to a variable.

A casting command looks like this.

```
var = int(var)
```

Instead of *var*, use the name of any variable. This command converts the variable to integer data type and stores the result using the same variable name. It overwrites the old variable with a new integer value.

```
age = int(age)
```

Sequence

An algorithm sets out the steps to transform inputs and create outputs. The simplest structure for an algorithm is a **sequence** of commands.

A sequence is a linear series of commands. The commands in the sequence will be carried out one at a time in the order they are given in the algorithm.

When you set out an algorithm it is important to get the sequence right. If one command uses the results of another, it must come after it in the sequence. One command *depends on* the other.

An algorithm with a sequence of commands is called a **sequential algorithm**.

You can show a sequential algorithm as text. For example, you can set out the algorithm using Exam Reference Language. Write the commands in the order they should be carried out.

Knowledge

20 Inputs and outputs

Sequence

Worked example

Write an algorithm that takes a number as input, raises it to the power 3, then outputs the result. Include commands to change the data type of the input if required.

```
number = input("enter a number:")
...
print(result)
```

Remember the IPO model. The algorithm must have input and output commands. You can use identifiers taken from the question ('number as input' and 'output the result').

You must add some processing commands between the input and the output. These commands must transform the input value to make the output.

```
result = number ^ 3
```

The commands must raise one number to the power of another. The exponentiation operator ^ does this.

```
number = int(number)
```

The exponentiation operator needs numerical data. So the input must be cast to a numerical data type.

Remember the sequence. The calculation *depends on* having a number value. The casting operation *creates* the number value. That means the casting operation must come before the calculation.

Following this structure, the full answer is:

```
number = input("enter a number")
number = int(number)
result = number ^ 3
print(result)
```

Sequential flowcharts

You can show a sequential algorithm using a flowchart. The arrows of the flowchart show the sequence of the algorithm.

This flowchart shows the algorithm to raise a number to the power 3.

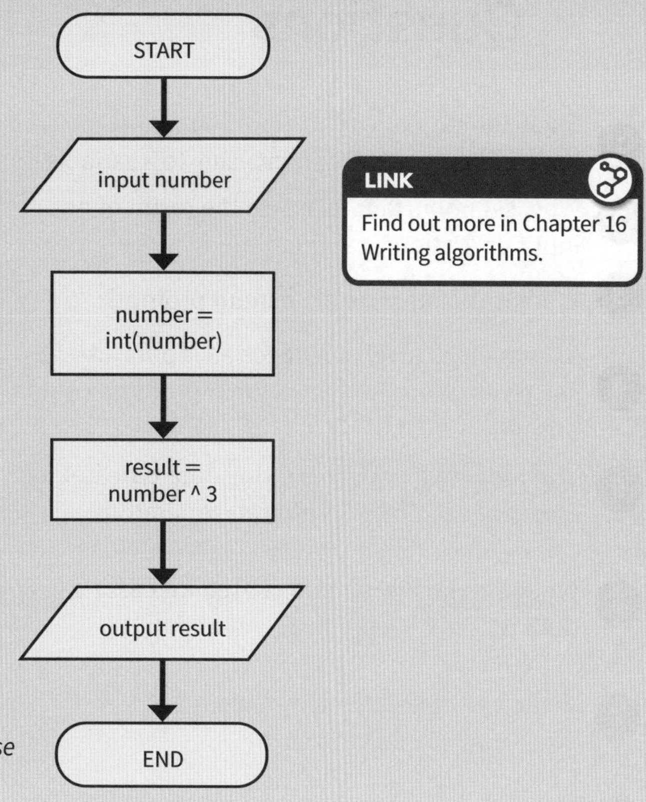

▶ ***Figure 2*** *Flowchart for a sequential algorithm to raise a number to the power 3*

LINK

Find out more in Chapter 16 Writing algorithms.

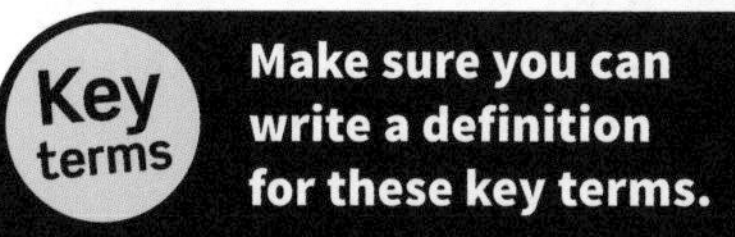

casting input output processing sequence sequential algorithm

Retrieval

Learn the answers to the questions below, then cover the answers column with a piece of paper and write down as many answers as you can. Check and repeat.

	Questions	Answers
1	Show the structure of an input command. Include the prompt. Assign the input value to a variable.	`variable = input(prompt)`
2	Why is it important to assign the result of an input operation to a variable?	assigning a value to a variable saves the value; if an input is not assigned to a variable, it will be lost
3	What is the purpose of an input prompt?	to tell the user what input is required by the program
4	In some high level languages all inputs are stored as string data type. What problem could arise from this?	when input values are stored as string data type they cannot be used in expressions with arithmetic operators
5	What must be done to a string data type before it can be used by an arithmetic operator?	it must be cast to a numerical data type

6	What are the five functions used for casting data type?	`int()`
		`real()` or `float()`
		`string()`
		`Boolean()`

7	What is result of this command? `print(expression)`	the computer evaluates the expression and outputs the result to the screen
8	What does it mean if an algorithm is sequential?	a sequential algorithm is a series of commands; the commands will be carried out one at a time in the order they are given in the algorithm
9	How is the sequence of an algorithm shown in a flowchart?	the arrows of the flowchart show the sequence of the commands
10	Explain how understanding dependency can help you to put commands in the correct sequence.	if one command is dependent on the result of another command, it must come after that command in the sequence of the algorithm

Put paper here

Previous questions

Now go back and use the questions below to check your knowledge from previous chapters.

	Previous questions	Answers
1	In a computational problem, how are inputs linked to outputs?	in a computational problem you can get from the inputs to the outputs using logical or mathematical steps
2	What are the four stages of the fetch-execute cycle?	fetch, decode, execute, store
3	State the part(s) of the processor where each stage of the fetch-execute cycle takes place.	fetch – memory and control unit; decode – control unit; execute – ALU; store – ALU and memory
4	Explain what happens to the data and instructions in storage when the electricity is turned off.	data and instructions are held in storage without being lost if the electricity is turned off
5	What are the three types of operator?	arithmetic, comparison, and Boolean

Put paper here

Exam-style questions

Devonte wants to write a program that allows three numbers to be input, then finds and outputs the total of these numbers followed by the average of these numbers.

EXAM TIP 

Questions of this type may be in either Section A or Section B. If it is in Section B, you *must* answer using either the OCR Exam Reference Language or a high level programming language you have studied. Follow this rule if the question is in Section A unless the question asks for a specific method of answering, such as a flowchart.

1 Write an algorithm to perform the following steps in the given order:

- ask the user to input three numbers
- input three numbers
- calculate the total of the three numbers
- output the total
- calculate the average of the three numbers
- output the average. **[6]**

2 Devonte wants to change the data type of data currently held in the variable should be `value` to the string data type and hold it in the variable `newvar`.

Write a program statement to perform this casting operation. **[1]**

3 Draw a flowchart to represent the algorithm in **question 1**. **[5]**

EXAM TIP 

Flowcharts must be drawn using the correct standard flowchart symbols.

Knowledge

21 Selection structure

Decisions in algorithms

A sequential algorithm completes the same actions every time. Sometimes programmers need an algorithm to include a choice between different actions. This is called a **selection** structure.

The choice of action is controlled by a logical test. That is a test which can be True or False.

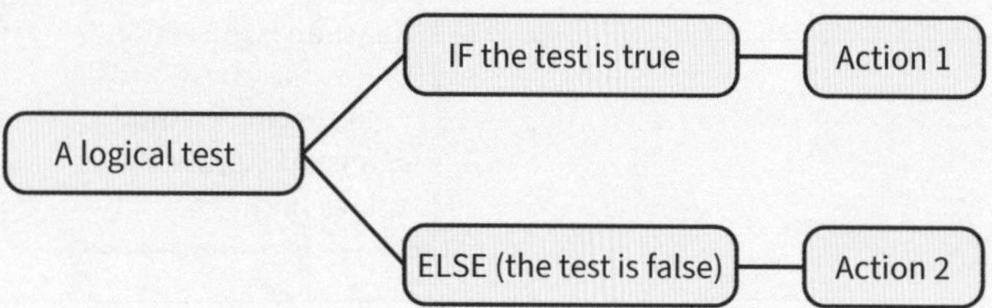

A logical test
IF the test is true
Action 1
ELSE (the test is false)
Action 2

▲ ***Figure 1*** *A selection structure*

A logical test is the same as a Boolean expression. A logical test compares two values. The comparison is either True or False.

LINK

Find out more in Chapter 18 Values and variables.

In a flowchart algorithm

A logical test in a flowchart is shown inside a diamond-shaped box.

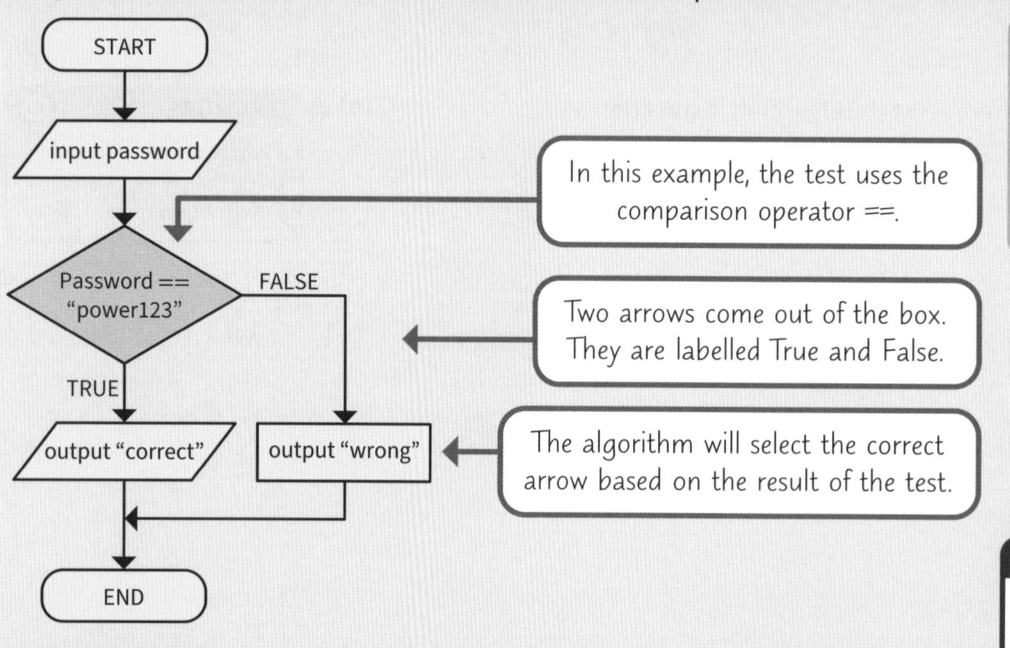

START
input password
Password == "power123"
FALSE
TRUE
output "correct"
output "wrong"
END
In this example, the test uses the comparison operator ==.
Two arrows come out of the box. They are labelled True and False.
The algorithm will select the correct arrow based on the result of the test.

▲ ***Figure 2*** *A selection structure in a flowchart*

REVISION TIP

Although the flowchart divides into two sets of arrows, all the arrows must join up again, and only one arrow enters the end box.

LINK

Find out more in Chapter 19 Operators.

In a text-based algorithm

In most high level languages, a selection structure is made using the keywords **`if`** and **`else`**.

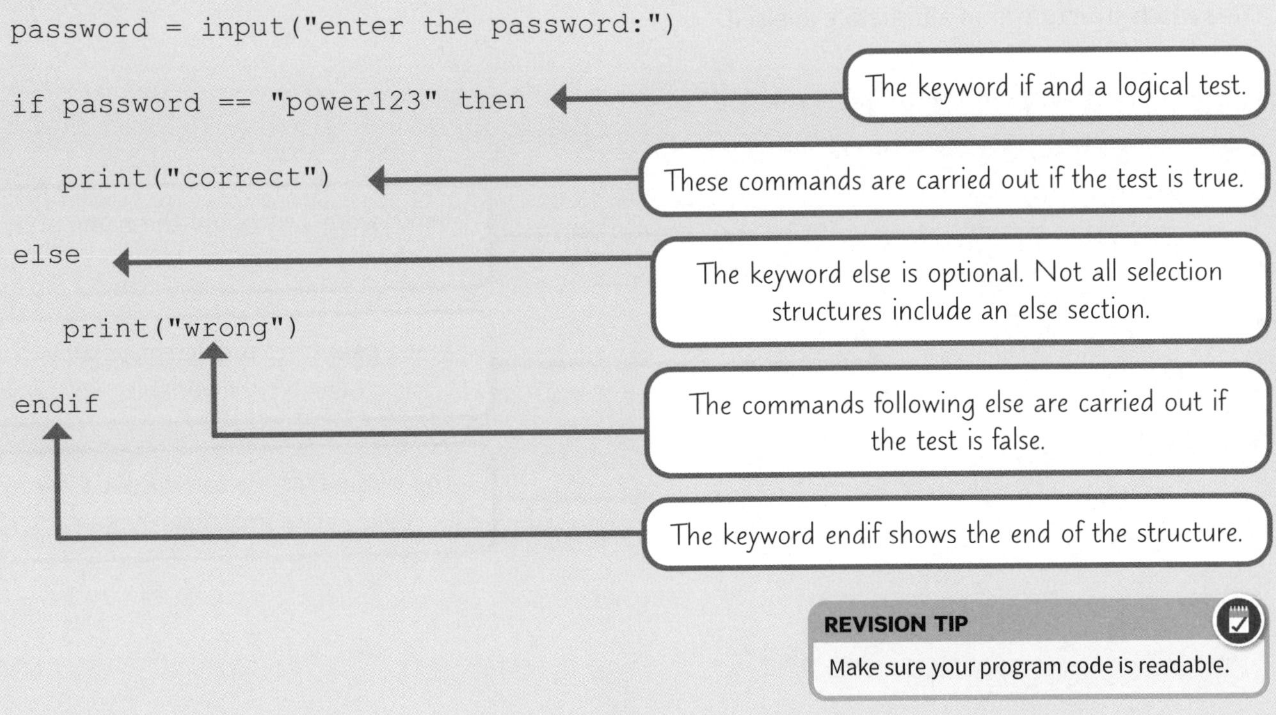

password = input("enter the password:")
if password == "power123" then
print("correct")
else
print("wrong")
endif
The keyword if and a logical test.
These commands are carried out if the test is true.
The keyword else is optional. Not all selection structures include an else section.
The commands following else are carried out if the test is false.
The keyword endif shows the end of the structure.

REVISION TIP

Make sure your program code is readable.

Elseif

Sometimes you might need to include more than one test in the same structure.

In this case you can use the keyword **`elseif`**.

REVISION TIP

Practise using the program structures shown in this section using a programming language you have learned.

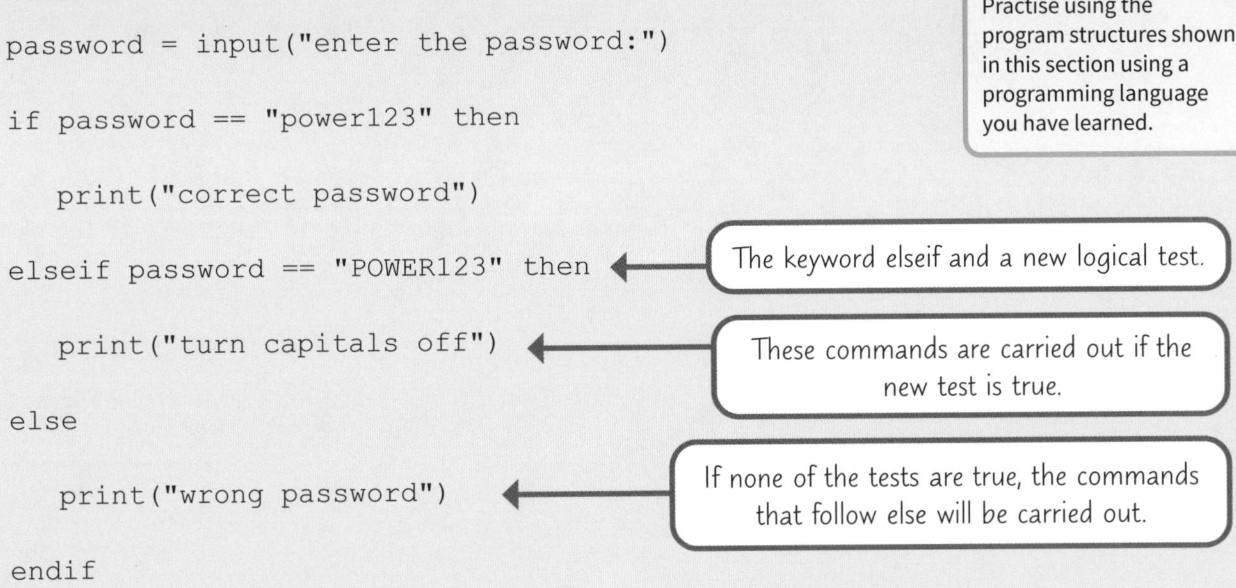

There can be one or more elseif lines. The program will go through all the tests in the structure until it finds a test that is True.

Knowledge

21 Selection structure

Switch

The **switch** structure is an alternative to elseif.

```
password = input("enter the password:")

switch password:

    case "power123":

        print("correct password")

    case "POWER123":

        print("turn capitals off")

    default

        print("wrong password")

endswitch
```

The keyword switch and the name of a variable.

Each **case** gives a different possible value for the variable.

The commands are carried out if the case matches.

If none of the cases match, the commands that follow **default** are carried out.

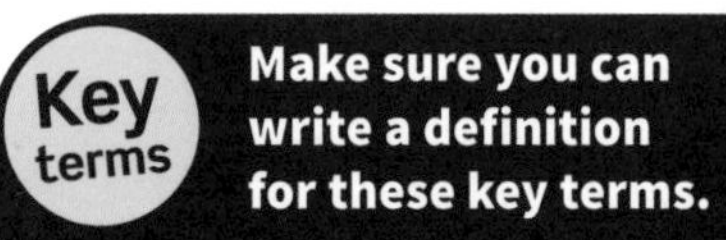
Key terms
Make sure you can write a definition for these key terms.

case default else elseif if indented selection switch

Indentation

The commands inside the selection structure are **indented**. That means there is a long space before them. They don't line up with the other commands.

- Indentation makes it easier to read a program. That is because it is easier to see which commands belong inside the structure.
- The indentation marks the start and end of the selection structure.
- Indentation is not only used to make the program more readable. In some languages, indentation is needed to make the program work correctly. Python is a language that uses indentation like this.
- Indentation is also used to show loop structures.

LINK 

Find out more in Chapter 22 Iteration (loop structures).

REVISION TIP 

If you have used a selection structure, include indentation to make the code readable.

Retrieval

Learn the answers to the questions below, then cover the answers column with a piece of paper and write down as many answers as you can. Check and repeat.

	Questions	Answers
1	What is the name of a structure that begins with the keyword 'if'?	a structure that begins with the keyword 'if' is called a selection structure
2	The keyword 'if' is followed by a logical test. What are the possible values of a logical test?	a logical test can have the values True or False
3	The keyword 'if' is followed by a logical test. How does the logical test control the flow of the program?	if the test is True, the commands that follow the test will be carried out; if the test is False these commands will not be carried out
4	How is a logical test shown in a flowchart algorithm? What is the shape of the box?	in a flowchart a logical test is shown by a decision box which is a diamond shape
5	What is indentation?	indentation means that lines of code are inset from the left margin
6	A selection structure can include the keyword 'else'. Explain how the keyword 'else' controls the flow of a program.	commands that follow the keyword 'else' are carried out if the logical test is false
7	A selection structure can include more than one logical test. Explain what keyword can be used in this case, and how it is used.	use the keyword 'elseif'; each 'elseif' is followed by a different logical test; the commands that follow each 'elseif' are caried out if the logical test is true
8	A different type of selection structure can be made using the keywords 'switch' and 'case'. What follows the keyword switch?	the keyword 'switch' is followed by the name of a variable
9	How is the keyword 'case' used?	the keyword 'case' is followed by a possible value of the variable; if this matches the real value of the variable, then the commands are carried out
10	How does indentation help make a program more readable?	it marks the start and end of a program structure, to show which commands belong inside

Put paper here

Previous questions

Now go back and use the questions below to check your knowledge from previous chapters.

	Previous questions	Answers
1	Why is it important to assign the result of an input operation to a variable?	assigning a value to a variable saves the value; if an input is not assigned to a variable, it will be lost
2	How is the sequence of an algorithm shown in a flowchart?	the arrows of the flowchart show the sequence of the commands
3	What does a compiler do?	a compiler reads the whole program and turns it into machine code, making a new file
4	What is the advantage of writing an algorithm using a flowchart instead of pseudocode?	a flowchart algorithm may be easier to understand, especially if you are a visual thinker

Put paper here

Practice

Exam-style questions

1 State the purpose of each of the comparison operators in the table.

Operator	Purpose
>	
!=	
<=	

[3]

2 Write an algorithm:

- to ask the user to input a whole number
- to perform a test to see if the number entered is an even number
- if the number is even, output a message that includes the number and states it is even
- to output an alternative suitable message of the number is not even. **[6]**

3 An algorithm is required to test whether a number that has been input is 50 or more. It should:

- input a number
- decide if this number is 50 or more
- output the result.

Design the algorithm using a flowchart. **[4]**

4 Write an algorithm that:

- asks the user to input a whole number between 1 and 4, inclusive
- if 1 is input, outputs the symbol '+'
- if 2 is input, outputs the symbol '–'
- if 3 is input, outputs the symbol '*'
- if 4 is input, outputs the symbol '/'
- if anything else is input, output an appropriate error message. **[6]**

EXAM TIP 

This question states that a flowchart is required, so you must answer with a flowchart.

EXAM TIP 

A question like **question 2** or **question 4** could be in either Section A or Section B. If it is in Section A and no specific method of answering is stated, any method, including a flowchart, may be used. Flowcharts must include the correct standard symbols.

If it is in Section B, you *must* answer using either the OCR Exam Reference Language or a high level programming language you have studied.

Knowledge

22 Iteration (loop structures)

Repeated commands

Many algorithms include **iteration**.

Iteration is also called a **loop structure**. One or more commands can be put inside a loop structure. These commands will be repeated until the loop stops.

REVISION TIP

Iteration means repetition.

Stop the loops

Commands inside a loop will repeat. There must be a way to stop the loop. Otherwise the commands will repeat forever.

An endless loop – a loop that does not stop – is a program error.

LINK

Find out more in Chapter 23 Coding errors.

There are different ways to stop a loop:

- **Condition-controlled** loops are stopped using a logical test that can be true or false.
- **Count-controlled loops** stop when they have repeated a set number of times.

You can use a count-controlled loop if you know exactly how many repeats you want in your program. If you do not know, then use a condition-controlled loop.

Loop in a flowchart

This flowchart shows an algorithm with a loop in it. The loop is controlled by a logical test.

In this example, the input command is inside the loop.

- The commands inside the loop will repeat until the test is True.
- When the test is True the loop will stop.

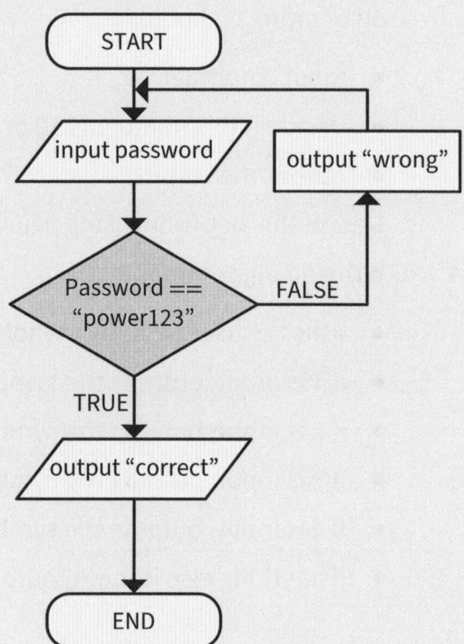

▶ ***Figure 1*** *If the test is false the arrow goes upwards, and the input command is repeated*

While loop

A condition-controlled loop can be defined using the keyword `while`.

```
password = input("enter the password:")

while password != "power123"

   password = input("try again:")

endwhile
```

At the start of the loop the computer tries the logical test. The operator != means not equal to.

The commands between while and endwhile are inside the loop. These are the commands that will be repeated.

If the test is True the commands inside the loop are carried out. If the test is False the loop will stop. The commands inside the loop will not be carried out.

The command inside the loop has been indented to improve readability.

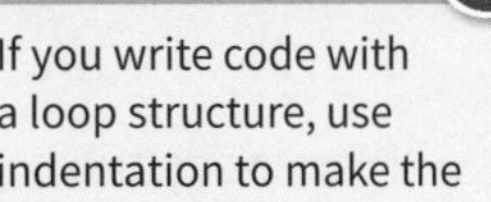

REVISION TIP

If you write code with a loop structure, use indentation to make the code readable.

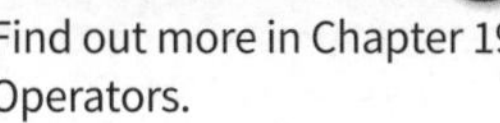

LINK

Find out more in Chapter 19 Operators.

Until loop

Another type of condition-controlled loop uses the keyword `until`.

In this type of loop the logical test is at the end of the loop. Here is an example of an until loop.

```
do
   password = input("enter the password:")
until password == "power123"
```

The commands between do and until are inside the loop. These are the commands that will be repeated.

If the test is True the loop stops. The loop will repeat if the test at the end is False.

In this type of loop the commands inside the loop will always be carried out at least once because the test doesn't happen until the end of the loop.

Knowledge

22 Iteration (loop structures)

For loop

Count-controlled loops start with the keyword `for`.

For loops include a variable called a counter. The variable stores the number of repeats.

The value of the counter typically starts at 0. Each time the program loops the counter increases by one. When the counter reaches the end value the loop stops.

```
for i = 0 to 4
    print("counting", i)
next i
```

The commands between for and next are inside the loop. These are the commands that will be repeated.

The commands inside the loop will repeat as the counter goes from 0 to 4.

The loop will repeat four times. This program will show these outputs:

```
counting 0
counting 1
counting 2
counting 3
```

When the counter reaches 4 the loop stops. So the value 4 is never printed out.

Many programmers use a lower-case i as the identifier of the counter variable.

Variations on the for loop

In the example above the counter starts at 0 and increases by 1 each time. Sometimes you don't want the counter to start at 0, or you don't want to count up in ones.

REVISION TIP 

Practise using the program structures shown in this section using a programming language you have learned.

This loop will count from 10 to 40 in steps of 10. It will print the values 10, 20 and 30.

```
for i = 10 to 40 step 10
    print(i)
next i
```

You can count backwards in steps of −1. This loop will count backwards from 10 to 1.

```
for i = 10 to 0 step -1
    print(i)
next i
```

Choice of loop

Understanding the different types of loop will help you to choose the right loop for every program you write.

Keyword	Type of loop	The loop stops when ...	Choose this loop when ...
while	condition-controlled loop	the test is False	you don't know how many repeats you need
until	condition-controlled loop	the test is True	you want the program to go through the loop at least once
for	count-controlled loop	the loop counter reaches a set value	you know how many times to repeat the loop

▲ ***Figure 2*** *Types of loop*

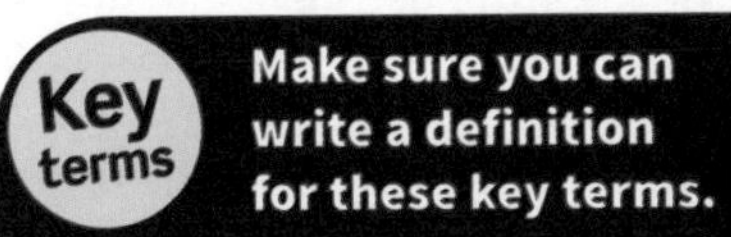
Key
terms
Make sure you can
write a definition
for these key terms.

condition-controlled loop   count-controlled loop   for loop   iteration   loop structure   until loop   while loop

Retrieval

Learn the answers to the questions below, then cover the answers column with a piece of paper and write down as many answers as you can. Check and repeat.

	Questions	Answers
1	A loop is a structure that includes repetition. What technical term is used to describe this type of structure?	iteration, or an iterative structure
2	Every loop must include a way to stop the repetition. What stops a condition-controlled loop from repeating?	a condition-controlled loop is stopped by a logical test (or Boolean expression)
3	A loop begins with the keyword 'while'. What controls the repetition of the loop?	the keyword 'while' is followed by a logical test; if True the commands inside the loop are carried out; if False the loop stops
4	A loop ends with the keyword 'until'. What controls the repetition of the loop?	the keyword 'until' is followed by a logical test; if True the loop stops; if False it repeats
5	What stops a count-controlled loop from repeating?	a counter records the number of repetitions; when the counter reaches a set value the loop stops
6	The header of a for loop begins with this code `for i =` What must follow this code?	it must be followed by: • the start value for the counter • the keyword 'do' • the stop value of the counter
7	A for loop may include the keyword 'step'. What happens if this keyword is not included?	if it is not included the counter increases by exactly one with each repetition of the loop
8	A for loop may include the keyword 'step'. What happens if this keyword is used?	the keyword 'step' is followed by a number; this number sets how much the counter variable will increase by each time the loop repeats
9	When would you use a condition-controlled loop in your program?	you would use a condition-controlled loop when you need commands to repeat, but you do not know how many times you want them to repeat
10	Some commands are included inside a while loop. The test at the top of the loop is false. How many more times will these commands be carried out?	if the test at the top of the while loop is false, the commands inside the loop will not be carried out at all

Put paper here

Previous questions

Now go back and use the questions below to check your knowledge from previous chapters.

	Previous questions	Answers
1	How does indentation help make a program more readable?	it marks the start and end of a program structure, to show which commands belong inside
2	The keyword 'if' is followed by a logical test. How does the logical test control the flow of the program?	if the test is True the commands that follow the test will be carried out; if the test is False these commands will not be carried out

Put paper here

Exam-style questions

1 Write an algorithm to:

- input 100 positive numbers
- add the numbers together as they are input
- output the total and average of these numbers once the inputs have been completed.

You must use **either**:

- OCR Exam Reference Language, or
- a high level language that you have studied. **[6]**

EXAM TIP

Make sure that you are aware of the three types of iteration and that you can construct algorithms in all three types.

2 The algorithm in **question 1** needs to be modified to allow any quantity of positive numbers to be input.

Write an algorithm to:

- input positive numbers until the value −1 is input
- add the numbers together as they are input
- record how many numbers have been input
- output the total and average of the numbers once −1 has been input.

You must use **either**:

- OCR Exam Reference Language, or
- a high level language that you have studied. **[6]**

EXAM TIP

When writing code with a loop structure, use indentation to make the code more readable.

3 Design an algorithm using a flowchart to:

- input a number
- test if the number is less than 100
- if it is, output a suitable message accepting the number
- if it is not, output a suitable error message and re-input the number. **[5]**

Knowledge

23 Coding errors

Error diagnostics

A programmer writes a program using an IDE (integrated development environment).

The IDE translates the program into machine readable form and runs the code.

Sometimes the program has errors in it. The IDE helps by identifying the error and showing an **error message**.

The error message says:

- what type of error the IDE has found
- where the error is in the program.

This process is called **error diagnostics**.

The programmer can then edit the code and remove the error. However, not all errors can be found by the IDE. That's why programs need to be tested before they are used in real life.

LINK
Find out more in Chapter 17 Programming languages.

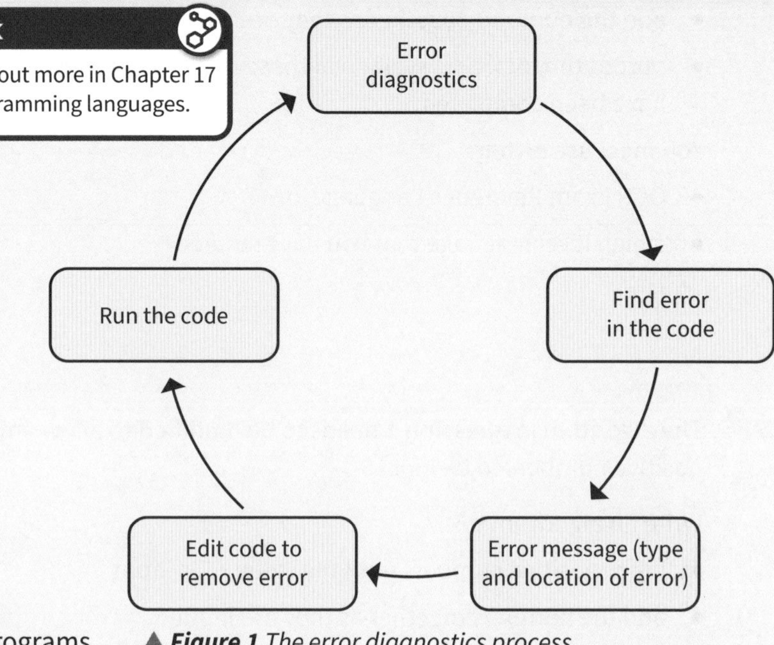

▲ ***Figure 1*** *The error diagnostics process*

Types of error

It is normal to make some errors when writing code. A good programmer works carefully to find and fix errors of all types.

There are three types of error:

- syntax errors
- run-time errors
- logical errors.

Each type of error is found in a different way.

Syntax errors

Syntax means the rules of a language. Programming languages such as Python and Java have syntax. When you write a program every line must follow the syntax of your chosen language. If the code breaks the rules of the language, that is a **syntax error**.

Some examples of syntax error:

- spelling program commands incorrectly
- putting commands in the wrong order
- mistakes with punctuation (such as not closing brackets).

Syntax errors

If the program has a syntax error, the IDE will not be able to translate the code.

- The translation process will halt.
- The IDE will show an error message.

The example in **Figure 2** is from the Python default IDE called IDLE.

In this example, the programmer has made an error in the header of a while loop.

The line should end with the colon symbol :

```
File  Edit  Format  Run  Options  Window  Help
metals = ["gold","silver","iron","copper"]
new = input("input a new metal: ")
while new != ""
    metals.append(new)
    new = input("input a new metal: ")
print(metals)
for i in range(len(metals)):
    print(metals[i])

SyntaxError
expected ':'
OK
```

▲ ***Figure 2** An example of a syntax error*

The error message identifies the location of the error. It says what the error is. Using this message the programmer can correct the error. Then the program will run.

Run-time errors

When all syntax errors have been fixed, the IDE can run the code, but the code might still have errors in it. These errors can make the program crash. This type of error is called a **run-time error**.

A run-time error happens when the program tries to make the computer do something impossible. For example:

- divide a number by zero
- try to carry out a calculation with a string variable.

```
x = 123
y = 0
print(x/y)
Traceback (most recent call last):
  File "<pyshell#2>", line 1, in <module>
    print(x/y)
ZeroDivisionError: division by zero
```

▲ ***Figure 3** A run-time error in the Python shell*

The IDE may spot run-time errors. The IDE will show a helpful error message.

Figure 3 shows an example from the Python shell.

In this example the three commands obey the rules of Python syntax. However, the third command asks the computer to divide 123 by 0. This is mathematically impossible, so there is a run-time error.

REVISION TIP

Introduce deliberate run-time errors and syntax errors into your code and make notes of how your IDE handles them. Use this information to revise for exam questions that ask about features of IDEs.

23 Coding errors

Logical errors

Error diagnostics help the programmer to remove syntax errors and run-time errors. Now the program will run. The computer can carry out all commands.

But sometimes the program does not do what you want it to. The program produces unwanted or unexpected output. This is called a **logical error**.

Error diagnostics will not find logical errors. That's because the computer does not know what you want the program to do.

Examples of logical error include:

- a computer game resets your score to zero for no reason
- a payroll program gives someone the wrong pay
- a self-driving car crashes into a wall.

To find logical errors, programs must be tested before they are used in real life.

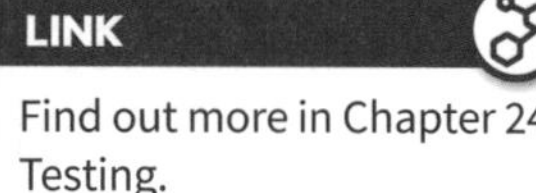

LINK

Find out more in Chapter 24 Testing.

Errors in algorithms

An algorithm sets out the logic of a program. But it is not a program. You cannot run an algorithm. You cannot use the error diagnostics of an IDE. This can make it harder to find errors in an algorithm.

In order to find errors in an algorithm you must use trace tables.

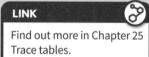

LINK

Find out more in Chapter 25 Trace tables.

User errors

Sometimes programs go wrong because of user error. The user enters the wrong inputs.

Programmers can try to avoid this problem by making programs user friendly. They can add validation to block incorrect inputs.

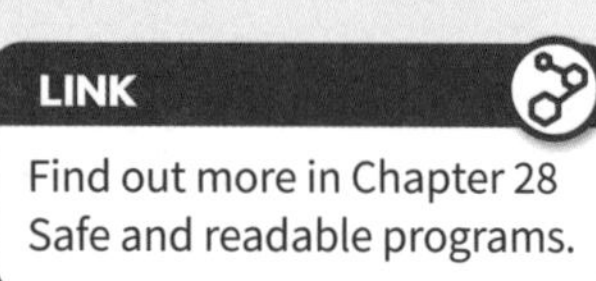

LINK

Find out more in Chapter 28 Safe and readable programs.

Key terms Make sure you can write a definition for these key terms.

error diagnostic   error message   logical error   run-time error   syntax   syntax error

Retrieval

Learn the answers to the questions below, then cover the answers column with a piece of paper and write down as many answers as you can. Check and repeat.

	Questions	Answers
1	What two pieces of information are provided by error diagnostics?	the location of an error in a program; the type of error
2	What is a syntax error?	a syntax error breaks the rules of a programming language
3	If a program has a syntax error the IDE cannot complete an important task. What task?	if there is a syntax error the IDE cannot translate the program into machine-readable form
4	A program includes a command to divide a number by zero. What type of error is this?	divide by zero is an example of a run-time error
5	Explain why a command to divide by zero causes an error.	the command is trying to make the computer do an impossible thing; the computer cannot complete this command so it causes an error
6	What is meant by a logical error?	a logical error means the program will run but the program will not do what you want it to
7	A program has a logical error. Why doesn't the computer show an error message?	the computer does not show an error message because it does not know what you want the program to do
8	What is the best way to find and fix the logical errors in a program?	the best way to find and fix logical errors is to test the program before it is used
9	A program includes a command to convert an input string of letters to the integer data type. What type of error is this?	a command to convert a value to the wrong data type is an example of a run-time error
10	A programmer spells a command word incorrectly. What type of error is this?	an incorrect spelling of a command word is an example of a syntax error

Put paper here

Previous questions

Now go back and use the questions below to check your knowledge from previous chapters.

	Previous questions	Answers
1	What stops a condition-controlled loop from repeating?	a condition-controlled loop is stopped by a logical test (or Boolean expression)
2	What stops a count-controlled loop from repeating?	a counter records the number of repetitions; when the counter reaches a set value the loop stops
3	What is the data type of an expression made using a comparison operator?	an expression made using a comparison operator is the Boolean data type
4	What are the key features of an IDE?	the key features of an IDE are editing tools, error diagnostics, a translator, and a run-time environment
5	What is the purpose of an input prompt?	to tell the user what input is required by the program

Put paper here

Practice

Exam-style questions

1 Outline the meaning of the terms syntax error **and** logic error **and** give an example of each error. **[4]**

> **EXAM TIP**
>
> Look at the features of the IDE that help you debug your programs and determine whether your errors are syntax errors or logic errors.

2 Explain the role of the IDE in finding and correcting errors in programs. **[3]**

3 A teacher has written an algorithm to add together 20 marks that are stored in the array marks. The array indexes run from 0 to 19.

After the marks have been added together the total of the marks is output.

The teacher has written the algorithm using the OCR Exam Reference Language:

```
sum = 0
counter = 1
while counter != 20
    sum = sum + marks[counter]
next counter
    counter = counter + 1
print(counter)
```

After testing, the algorithm has been found to contain **two** syntax errors and **two** logic errors.

Identify each of the errors and outline how each error can be corrected. **[4]**

> **EXAM TIP**
>
> Make sure that you clearly identify each error and how it can be corrected. Both parts are required.

24 Testing

Need for testing

Every program must be tested before it is used. That is to make sure the program works properly.

If the program still has errors when it is used in real life, this can cause significant issues.

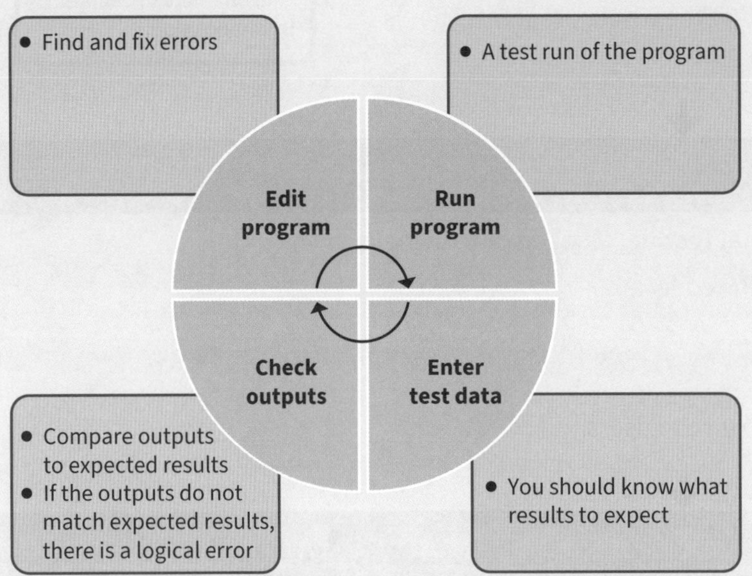

• Find and fix errors
• A test run of the program
Edit program
Run program
Check outputs
Enter test data
• Compare outputs to expected results
• If the outputs do not match expected results, there is a logical error
• You should know what results to expect

Figure 1 *The testing cycle*

LINK

Find out more in Chapter 23 Coding errors.

Some games companies ask users to help with testing.

The users will try out an unfinished version of the game. They will report any errors they find. This process is called beta testing.

Iterative testing

Iterative testing means testing a program during development. Iterative testing is repeated many times during the development of a program.

The process of iterative testing follows the overall plan shown in **Figure 2**.

1. Testing finds errors in the code.
2. The programmer fixes the errors.
3. Now the program should work correctly.
4. This means it is time to test the code again.
5. The process is repeated until there are no more errors.

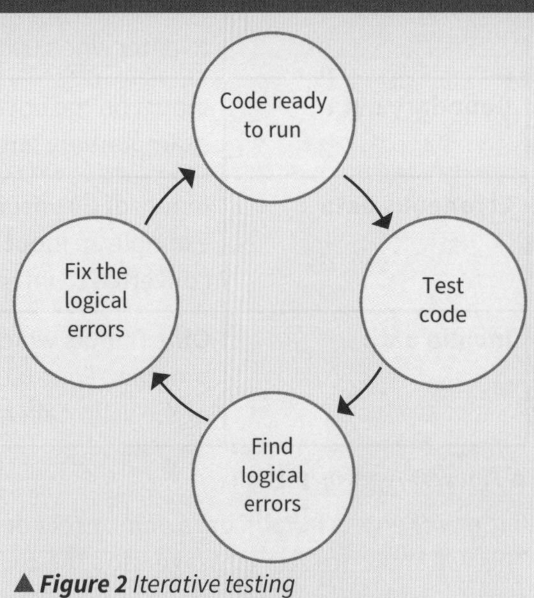

Code ready to run
Test code
Find logical errors
Fix the logical errors

Figure 2 *Iterative testing*

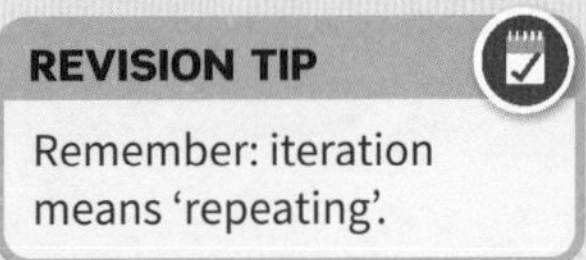

REVISION TIP

Remember: iteration means 'repeating'.

Knowledge

24 Testing

Modular testing

Iterative testing can be modular. **Modular testing** means testing the modules of a program. Modules are the functions and procedures used in the program. A module should be tested to make sure it has no errors. Then the module can be used in a program.

Testing a module is quicker and easier than testing the whole program. That is because a module is shorter and simpler than a program.

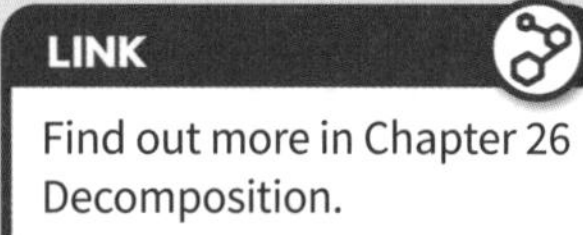

LINK

Find out more in Chapter 26 Decomposition.

Final testing

As well as iterative testing, programmers use **final testing**. Final testing is when:

- the programmers have finished developing the code
- the program is ready to be used or sold
- the whole program is tested, not just modules.

Final testing checks that the program is ready to give to users.

Test data

Test data means the inputs used in testing. The programmer must use a wide range of test data.

Figure 3 shows the different types of test data that a programmer should use. Both iterative and final testing should include all these types of test data.

Type of test data	What it means	Expected output
Normal data	The normal inputs you would expect users to enter when using this program	Input accepted with no error and program continues
Boundary data	Inputs on the edge of being incorrect (for example, very large or small values)	Input accepted with no error and program continues
Erroneous data	Inputs of the incorrect data type. For example an input string which cannot be converted to integer	Input rejected by the program
Invalid data	Other inputs which are not allowed by the program. For example, numbers outside of the valid data range.	Input rejected by the program

▲ ***Figure 3*** *Types of test data*

If the user enters **invalid data** or incorrect data the program should reject the data. This will show an error message, stop the program, or ask for the input again.

Make and use a test plan

A test plan sets out the tests you plan to do.

Before you start testing you must set out:

- **type of test**: the test plan should include all types of data
- **test data**: what inputs you will use
- **expected outputs**: what you should see if the program works correctly.

After the test is done, complete the test plan:

- **actual outputs**: for example, a screen shot
- **analysis**: do the actual and expected results match? If not, there is a program error.

REVISION TIP 

Practise creating your own test plans for different scenarios.

Figure 4 shows part of a test plan. In this example, it is testing a module where the user must enter their age. If they are within the correct range, the program applies a student discount.

Type of test	Test data	Expected output	Actual output	Analysis
Normal	16	Accepted – Student discount applied	Student discount applied	Program works
Boundary	0	Accepted – No discount applied	No discount applied	Program works
Erroneous	"ab"	Rejected – Error message	Error message	Program works
Invalid	−65	Rejected – Error message	Input is accepted	LOGICAL ERROR FOUND

▲ ***Figure 4*** *An example test plan*

Key terms
Make sure you can write a definition for these key terms.

boundary data erroneous data final testing invalid data iterative testing modular testing normal data test data

Learn the answers to the questions below, then cover the answers column with a piece of paper and write down as many answers as you can. Check and repeat.

	Questions	Answers
1	One type of program error can only be found by testing. What type?	logical errors can only be found by testing
2	In a test, what does the programmer compare the actual outputs to?	the programmer compares the actual outputs to the expected outputs
3	What is iterative testing and how often is it carried out during the development process?	iterative testing means repeated testing; it is repeated many times during development
4	Iterative testing often includes modular testing. What is modular testing?	modular testing means testing the parts of a program, such as the procedures and functions used in the program
5	What is the advantage of modular testing?	it can be easier to carry out modular testing, and to find and fix errors, because a module is shorter and simpler than the whole program
6	What is final testing?	final testing is carried out once at the end of program development; it is the final check to make sure there are no errors before the program is used
7	What are test data?	test data are the pretend inputs entered during testing
8	What are the main types of test data?	test data should include normal, boundary, invalid, and erroneous data
9	A test plan sets out the test data the programmer plans to use. What other information is put into the test plan?	the test plan should set out the expected output of each test
10	After the test is completed, extra information is added to the test plan. What extra information is added?	after the test is finished, the programmer adds the actual output produced during the test, and compares it to the expected result

Put paper here

Previous questions

Now go back and use the questions below to check your knowledge from previous chapters.

	Previous questions	Answers
1	If a program has a syntax error the IDE cannot complete an important task. What task?	if there is a syntax error, the IDE cannot translate the program into machine-readable form
2	A program includes a command to divide a number by zero. What type of error is this?	divide by zero is an example of a run-time error
3	What is the meaning of the comparison operator !=?	the comparison operator != means 'not equal to'; the expression is True if the values are not equal
4	What does it mean if an algorithm is sequential?	it is a series of commands that will be carried out one at a time in the order they are given

Put paper here

Exam-style questions

1 Describe iterative testing **and** terminal/final testing. **[4]**

2 Identify **one** advantage of modular iterative testing over terminal testing. **[1]**

EXAM TIP

Practice identifying different types of test data and suggesting items of test data for the programs you write.

3 A test is performed on the input of data to make sure that it is an integer between 1 and 1000, inclusive.

Tick (✓) **one or more** boxes in each row to identify the type of test data each piece of test data represents.

	Type of test data		
Test data	**Normal**	**Boundary**	**Erroneous**
1			
500.78			
499			
Fifty			

[4]

4 A ticket sales app allows users to buy between one and five tickets for a concert.

Complete the test plan to check whether the program correctly accepts or rejects the number of tickets input.

Test data (number of tickets)	Type of test	Expected output
two		
	Boundary	
		Accepted
		Rejected

[4]

EXAM TIP

Test plans can include more columns than this to fully document actual tests you have carried out when creating your program.

Knowledge

25 Trace tables

Purpose

Programmers use algorithms to plan and share program ideas. An algorithm is not written in a programming language. It cannot be translated into machine code. It cannot run on a computer.

LINK

Find out more in Chapter 16 Writing algorithms.

Testing a program means running the program and looking at the outputs.

You cannot test an algorithm in this way. Instead the programmer must **trace the algorithm**. That means going through the algorithm on paper.

All types of algorithm can be traced.

- Trace a text-based algorithm line by line.
- Trace a flowchart algorithm by following the arrows from box to box.

Test inputs are used, in the same way as for testing a program.

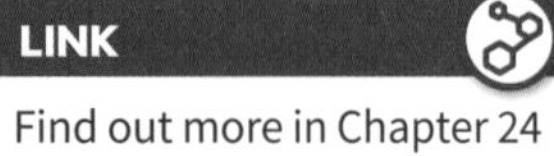

LINK

Find out more in Chapter 24 Testing.

The test inputs set the starting values for all variables used in the algorithm.

The purpose of tracing is to find logical errors in the algorithm. Or to find out what the algorithm does.

Trace an algorithm

To trace an algorithm:

Create an empty **trace table**. → Go through the algorithm line by line. → At the end you will note what the outputs are.

Make an empty trace table

To trace an algorithm you must identify all the variables used in the algorithm.

Read through the algorithm and note the names of all the variables.

LINK

Find out more in Chapter 18 Values and variables.

Make an empty table with a column for each variable in the algorithm. There should also be a column for line number and a column for outputs.

Go through line by line

To trace the algorithm go through it line by line. As you trace the algorithm, fill in the trace table.

- At each line, fill in the line number and the value of each variable at that line.
- If a line assigns input to a variable, use the test inputs that you planned in advance.
- If a value of a variable does not change then copy the value from the line above.

When the trace table is completed, it will show the outputs of the algorithm.

Compare the actual and expected outputs. They should match. If they do not match there are errors in the algorithm.

Make sure you can write a definition for these key terms.

trace an algorithm   trace table

Go through line by line

Worked example

Trace this algorithm. Show the output when the numbers 16 and 2 are input.

```
1 num1 = input()
2 num2 = input()
3 num1 = num1/num2
4 result = num1 ^ num2
5 print(result)
```

The algorithm has three variables: num1, num2, and result.

The empty trace table looks like this.

line	num1	num2	result	output

In the first two lines the input values 16 and 2 are assigned to the variables num1 and num2.

line	num1	num2	result	output
1	16			
2	16	2		

line	num1	num2	result	output
1	16			
2	16	2		
3	8	2		

At line 3 the value of num1 is divided by num2. 16 ÷ 2 is 8, so change the value of num1 to 8. The value of num2 does not change.

Now go through the algorithm line by line, showing the value of each variable at each line.

Here is the completed trace table.

line	num1	num2	result	output
1	16			
2	16	2		
3	8	2		
4	8	2	64	
5	8	2	64	64

The output of the algorithm is the number 64.

Watch out for loops and ifs

Some algorithms have if or loop structures. In this case, do not go through the algorithm line by line from top to bottom. Instead follow the logic of the structure. Jump forward or back in the algorithm according to the commands.

Retrieval

Learn the answers to the questions below, then cover the answers column with a piece of paper and write down as many answers as you can. Check and repeat.

	Questions	Answers
1	Programs should be tested by running the program on a computer. But algorithms are not tested in this way. Why not?	algorithms are not written in a programming language; they cannot be run on a computer
2	Before you trace a program, you should note all the identifiers. What identifiers?	you should note the identifiers of all variables used in the algorithm
3	What column headings are used in a trace table?	line number; identifiers of all variables; output
4	A pseudocode algorithm is traced line by line. How is a flowchart algorithm traced?	trace a flowchart algorithm by following the arrows from shape to shape
5	What values do you put into the trace table as you trace the algorithm?	fill in the value that each variable holds at each line of the program
6	A line of an algorithm assigns an input value to a variable. How do you know what value to give to that variable?	use the test data values that you planned in advance
7	A line of an algorithm does not change the value of a variable. What value do you put into the trace table?	copy the value from the previous line of the trace table, with no change
8	How can you use tracing to find errors in an algorithm?	before you trace the algorithm, you should decide on the expected outputs; compare actual and expected outputs; if they do not match there is an error in the algorithm

Put paper here

Previous questions

Now go back and use the questions below to check your knowledge from previous chapters.

	Previous questions	Answers
1	What are test data?	test data are the pretend inputs entered during testing
2	What are the main types of test data?	test data should include normal, boundary, invalid, and erroneous data
3	What are the numerical data types?	the numerical data types are integer and real (or float)
4	What is the difference between the numerical data types?	integers are whole numbers; reals can include a decimal point
5	When would you use a condition-controlled loop in your program?	you would use a condition-controlled loop when you need commands to repeat, but you do not know how many times you want them to repeat

Put paper here

Practice

Exam-style questions

1 The following algorithm allows a teacher to input 30 test scores. It will then total these scores and output the average.

```
01 total = 0
02 print("Input each test score when prompted")
03 for count = 1 to 30
04     print("Test score " + count)
05     score = input()
06     total = total + score
07 next count
08 print("Average score = " + total / 30)
```

Write the first row of the trace table for this algorithm to show the appropriate column headings. You do not need to trace the algorithm. **[3]**

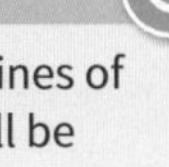

EXAM TIP

In the exam the lines of the algorithm will be numbered.

2 A Fibonacci sequence is a mathematical series of numbers. The first eight numbers in the sequence are:

0, 1, 1, 2, 3, 5, 8, 13

The following algorithm takes a number as input. It outputs the Fibonacci number at that position in the sequence.

```
01  fib = 0
02  f0 = 0
03  f1 = 1
04  n = input("Input a number: ")
05  if n == 2 then
06      fib = 1
07  endif
08  count = 2
09  while count < n
10      fib = f0 + f1
11      f0 = f1
12      f1 = fib
13      count = count + 1
14  endwhile
15  print("The Fibonacci number at position " + n + "
    is " + fib)
```

EXAM TIP

The number of rows in a table in the exam should be sufficient for you to complete the trace, but if you run out of space, make sure your continuation is clear.

EXAM TIP

Try tracing this algorithm for different values of n.

Complete the following trace table for the input data: 5.

line number	fib	f0	f1	n	count	output
01	0					
02		0				

[6]

Knowledge

26 Decomposition

Breaking a problem down

Programmers often have to write complex programs, to solve difficult problems. To make this easier they can break the big problem down into smaller parts. This is called **decomposition**.

Decomposition has many benefits.

- Smaller problems are easier to solve.
- Smaller programs are easier to write and test.
- The parts can be divided between a team of programmers to share the work.

The smaller parts of a large program can be called **sub programs**. A sub program is a block of code saved using an identifier. Two important types of sub program are **procedures** and functions. In this section you will learn about procedures.

Code that has been broken down into subsections is called **structured code**.

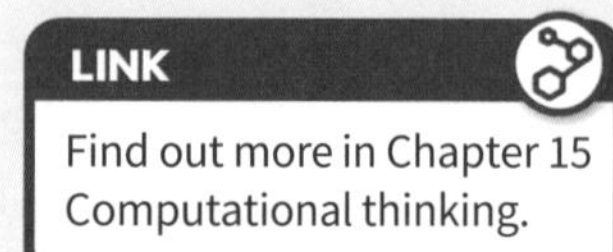

LINK
Find out more in Chapter 15 Computational thinking.

Structure diagram

A **structure diagram** can be used to show the sub programs that make up a program.

In the example in **Figure 1**, the program is a card game. It is broken down into three sub programs.

Some of the problems are still quite large so they can be broken down further.

In **Figure 2**, the sub program 'take turns' has been broken down into three smaller sub programs.

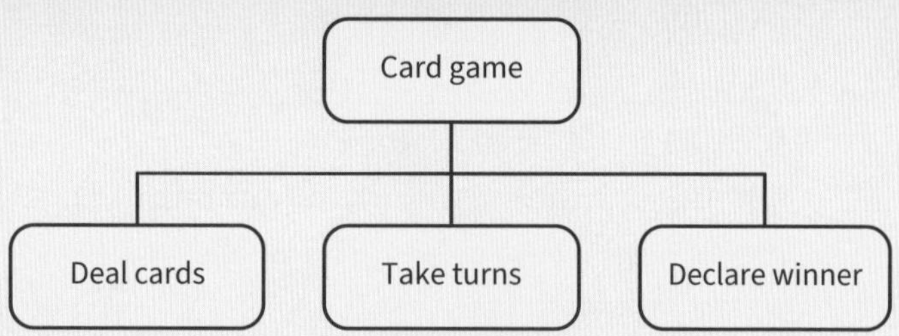

▲ ***Figure 1*** *The structure of a card game program*

▲ ***Figure 2*** *'Take turns' has been broken down into three smaller parts*

The rule is to break down the program until each sub program does one task, and one task only.

Flowchart diagram

A structure diagram in the card game example shows decomposition in parts. However, it does not show the flow of the program.

To do that you need to use a flowchart. In a flowchart, each sub program is shown in a box like the one in **Figure 3**.

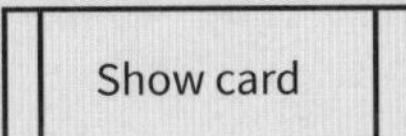

▲ ***Figure 3*** *A sub program box*

The name of the sub program is given in the box.

The flowchart in **Figure 4** shows how the sub programs link together.

Other flowcharts may be used to show the commands inside each sub program.

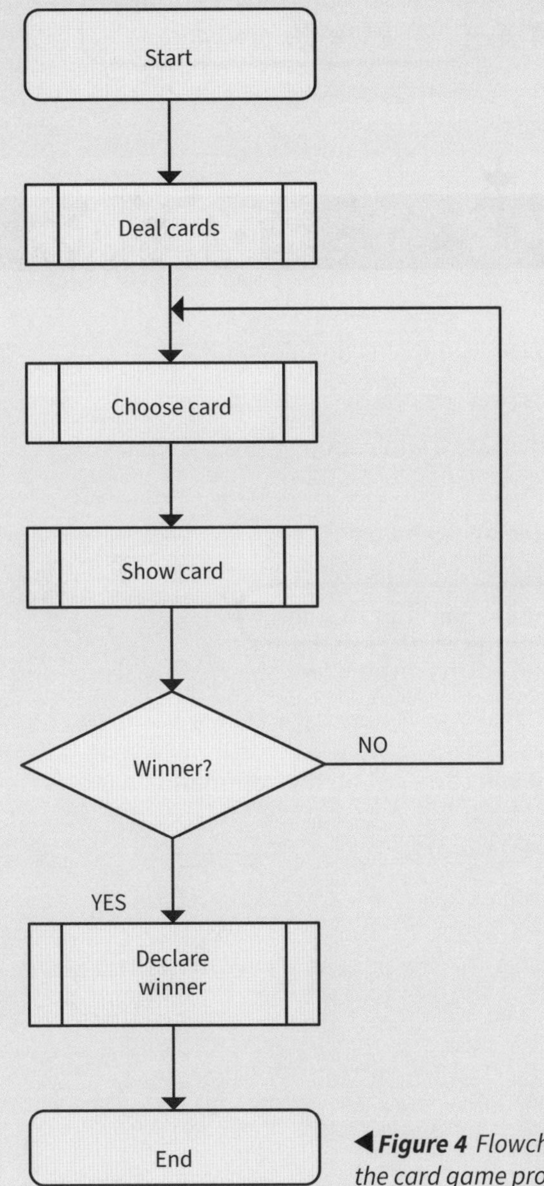

◀ ***Figure 4*** *Flowchart for the card game program*

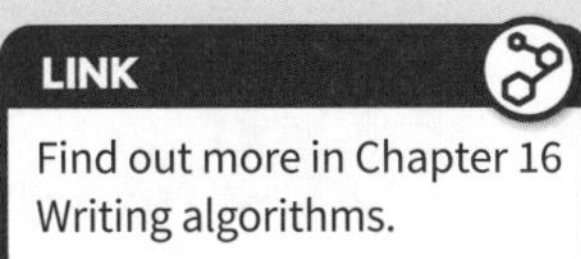

Find out more in Chapter 16 Writing algorithms.

26 Decomposition

Declare a procedure

One type of sub program is a **procedure**. Each procedure has a name (an identifier). Commands are stored inside the procedure.

The following procedure is called 'startscreen'. It shows the welcome message for a game called Cardmaster.

```
procedure startscreen()

    print("======================")

    print("welcome to card master")

    print("======================")

endprocedure
```

This is the header of the procedure. It shows the identifier.

These commands are stored inside the procedure.

Call a procedure

The procedure can be **called** inside the main program.

Calling a procedure means writing the name of the procedure, plus opening and closing brackets.

In this example, the procedure startscreen() is called inside a while loop.

```
continue = "N"
while continue == "N"
    startscreen()
    continue = input("do you wish to continue?")
endwhile
```

The procedure is called in this line.

When the computer comes to the procedure name, it will carry out all the commands in the procedure.

Naming for readability

Each procedure has a name (or identifier). Good identifiers make programs more readable. A good identifier will remind you of what the procedure does.

In most programming languages identifiers must be single words, with no spaces in them.

LINK 

Find out more in Chapter 28 Safe and readable programs.

Maintainable programming

After a program has been written, it might need to be changed. This might be to fix an error or add new features. Making these changes is called maintaining the program. A program that is easy to maintain is called a maintainable program.

Decomposition makes a program more maintainable. If a program is broken into sub programs it is:

- easier to read
- easier to change
- easier to test.

REVISION TIP 

Your understanding of these principles and how they are used will help you to define and refine problems.

LINK 

Find out more in Chapter 27 Procedures and functions.

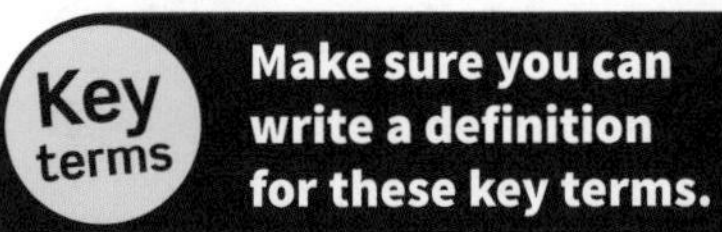
Key
terms
Make sure you can write a definition for these key terms.

called decomposition maintainable procedure structured code structure diagram sub program

Retrieval

Learn the answers to the questions below, then cover the answers column with a piece of paper and write down as many answers as you can. Check and repeat.

	Questions	Answers
1	What is decomposition?	breaking a large problem down into smaller parts
2	List three benefits of decomposition.	smaller problems are easier to solve; smaller programs are easier to write and test; the work of writing can be shared between a team of programmers
3	What is a sub program?	a group of commands saved using an identifier
4	What is the name for the style of programming that uses sub programs?	structured programming
5	What is the name of a chart that shows decomposition but not the flow of the program?	a structure diagram
6	Draw the type of box used in a flowchart to show a sub program.	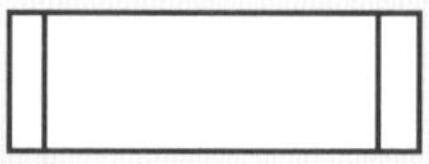 [box with double vertical lines at each side]
7	Write the first line of the code to define a procedure, using 'name' as the identifier of the procedure.	`procedure name()`
8	Write the final line of the code to define a procedure.	`endprocedure`
9	What is written inside a procedure, indented between the first and final lines?	all the commands that make up the procedure
10	How is a procedure called in the main program?	by writing the name of the procedure followed by opening and closing brackets

Put paper here

Previous questions

Now go back and use the questions below to check your knowledge from previous chapters.

	Previous questions	Answers
1	Programs should be tested by running the program on a computer. But algorithms are not tested in this way. Why not?	algorithms are not written in a programming language; they cannot be run on a computer
2	What values do you put into the trace table as you trace the algorithm?	fill in the value that each variable holds at each line of the program
3	Iterative testing often includes modular testing. What is modular testing?	modular testing means testing the parts of a program, such as the procedures and functions used in the program
4	What is the advantage of modular testing?	it can be easier to carry out modular testing, and to find and fix errors, because a module is shorter and simpler than the whole program
5	What is meant by a logical error?	a logical error means the program will run but the program will not do what you want it to

Put paper here

Exam-style questions

1 Define the term **decomposition**. [1]

2 A satellite television set top box has components to select a television programme to watch from a television guide, or from stored programmes on a hard drive. The programme can then be output either to a television screen, or to a recording device.

Complete the structure diagram to represent the satellite television set top box.

Satellite television set top box

[4]

EXAM TIP

Structure diagrams are usually expected to have a hierarchical layout.

3 Create a procedure, `errorMessage()`, that when called, displays a message to say an error has been made and waits for any key to be pressed before returning to the main program.

You must use **either**:

- OCR Exam Reference Language, or
- a high level language that you have studied. [3]

4 Create an algorithm that will check if a Boolean variable `flag` is true. If it is, the procedure `errorMessage()` is called.

You must use **either**:

- OCR Exam Reference Language, or
- a high level language that you have studied. [2]

5 Explain how the use of sub programs contributes to the maintainability of a program. [2]

EXAM TIP

List the different methods used to make a program maintainable and how you can improve your programs by using these techniques.

Knowledge

27 Procedures and functions

Types of sub program

Programs can be broken down into sub programs. There are two important types of sub program:

- **Procedures** carry out commands when called by the main program.
- **Functions** carry out commands and return a new value to the main program.

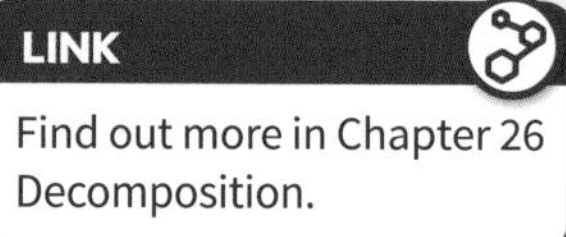

LINK

Find out more in Chapter 26 Decomposition.

Parameters

Procedures and functions may include one or more **parameters**.

This procedure with a parameter is called endscreen. The parameter is called winner.

```
procedure endscreen(winner)
   print("congratulations to", winner)
endprocedure
```

The identifier of the parameter is shown inside brackets in the first line of the subroutine.

The parameter can be used like a variable inside the subroutine.

Parameter values

The parameter is given a value when a procedure or function is called. The parameter value is shown in brackets. **Figure 1** shows two examples for the procedure endscreen().

Line in main program	What the procedure prints out
`endscreen("Sandy")`	`congratulations to Sandy`
`endscreen("Charlene")`	`congratulations to Charlene`

▲ ***Figure 1*** *Examples of parameter values*

The procedure uses the parameter value sent from the main program. The value of the parameter affects what the procedure does.

When you call a procedure or function, remember to check the first line of the subroutine:

- check how many parameters there are
- check the order of the parameters.

Make sure you provide the right number of values, in the right order.

REVISION TIP

When you call a sub program, make sure you give the right parameters, in the right order.

Functions

Functions are another type of sub program. A function **returns a value** to the main program.

Here is an example. This function is called 'square'. It returns a value called 'new'.

```
function square(number)
    new = number ** 2
    return new
endfunction
```

This sub program is a function. This value is returned to the main program.

You can call a function from the main program. You can choose the parameter value. The value of the parameter will affect the returned value.

Figure 2 shows two examples.

Function call with parameter	The returned value
square(4)	16
square(100)	10000

▲ ***Figure 2*** *Examples of returned parameter values*

REVISION TIP

If you see the code for a sub program, check for the keyword return. If a sub program returns a value it is a function. If it does not return a value it is a procedure.

Using functions

A function can be called in the main program, in the same way as a procedure. Write the name of the function followed by a pair of brackets. Write the parameter values inside the brackets. But remember that a function returns a value.

- The returned value can be used in a command. For example, it can be printed out.
- The returned value can be saved to use later, by assigning it to a variable.

In this example, the returned value is printed out:

```
print(square(100))
```

In this example, the returned value is assigned to a variable called result.

```
result = square(100)
```

If the returned value is not used or captured, then it will be lost by the program.

27 Procedures and functions

Local variables

Variables can be made and used inside a subroutine. If a variable is created inside a subroutine it is called a **local variable**.

```
function square(number)
    new = number ** 2
    return new
endfunction
```

New is a local variable.

A local variable can only be used inside that subroutine. If you try to use it in any other part of the program, it makes a syntax error.

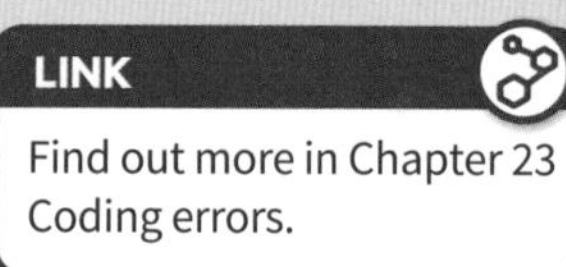

LINK

Find out more in Chapter 23 Coding errors.

Global variables

Sometimes a programmer wants to be able to use a variable anywhere in the program, in any procedure or function. In that case they can make it into a **global variable**.

```
procedure square(number)
    global new = number ** 2
endprocedure
```

New is a global variable.

A global variable can be used anywhere in the program with no syntax error.

There is no need to use a return command and there is no restriction on how many global values you can have.

However, many programmers avoid using global variables. A global variable may overwrite values in other parts of the program. This can cause unexpected side effects. Using global variables is risky. Using parameters and returned values is safer and more reliable.

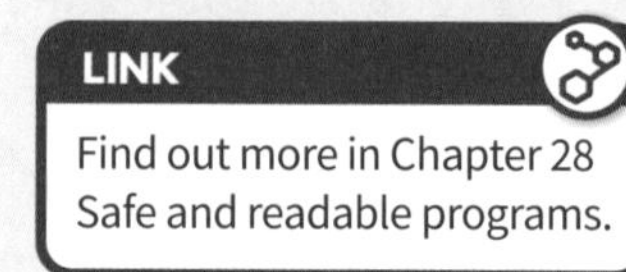

LINK

Find out more in Chapter 28 Safe and readable programs.

Predefined functions

Most programming languages include some ready-made functions. You can use these functions without defining them. They are called **predefined functions**.

If you use a predefined function you must:

- include any parameter values
- use or capture the returned value.

Random numbers

An example of a predefined function is the random() function.

This function returns a **random number** in a given range. A random number is an unpredictable number. It can fall anywhere in the range.

The function random() needs two parameters. These are numbers that set the range for the random number. Here is an example of the random function in use.

```
num = random(1,100)
```

This makes a random integer between 1 and 100. It assigns the returned value to the variable num.

If don't want an integer, you need to set the range using two numbers with a decimal point. If the numbers have a decimal point, then the random number will have a decimal point in it.

```
num = random(1.0,100.0)
```

Key terms — Make sure you can write a definition for these key terms.

function global variable local variable parameter predefined function procedure random number returned value

Retrieval

Learn the answers to the questions below, then cover the answers column with a piece of paper and write down as many answers as you can. Check and repeat.

	Questions	Answers
1	What is the difference between a procedure and a function?	a function returns a value, a procedure does not
2	A subroutine definition can include a parameter. How is the name of the parameter shown in the sub program definition?	the name of the parameter appears in brackets in the first line of the sub program definition
3	A sub program is called from the main program. How is the value of the parameter given in the main program?	the value of the parameter is given in brackets after the name of the sub program in the main program
4	How many parameter values must you include? How can you tell how many to use?	the number of parameter values you send must match the number of parameters in the subroutine definition
5	A function sends a value back to the main program. What command inside a function makes this happen?	the keyword 'return' followed by the value
6	The value can be used right away in the main program. What is the alternative to using the returned value right away?	the returned value can be assigned to a variable in the main program, to be used later
7	If a variable is defined inside a procedure or function, where can it be used? What is the name of this type of variable?	if a variable is defined inside a sub program, it can only be used inside that sub program; it is called a local variable
8	An alternative to returning a value is to use a global variable. What are the advantages of using global variables?	global variables can be used anywhere in the program without causing a syntax error; there is no restriction on the number of global variables
9	What are the disadvantages of using global variables?	global variables are seen as risky; they can overwrite values anywhere in the program, causing unwanted side effects
10	The predefined function `random()` requires two parameters. What is the purpose of these parameters?	the two parameters are numbers; they define a range of numbers; the random function returns a value from within this range

Put paper here

Previous questions

Now go back and use the questions below to check your knowledge from previous chapters.

	Previous questions	Answers
1	What is the name for the style of programming that uses sub programs?	structured programming
2	List three benefits of decomposition.	smaller problems are easier to solve; smaller programs are easier to write and test; writing can be shared between a team of programmers

Put paper here

Exam-style questions

1 Complete the table by writing the missing name or description for each programming feature related to procedures and functions.

Programming feature	Description
Function	
	A variable that can be used anywhere in the program
	A variable that can only be used inside the procedure or function in which it is created
Parameter	
Procedure	

[5]

EXAM TIP

Once you have completed this table, make sure you remember these terms to help with any practical tasks that may arise.

2 Create a function, `averageValue()`, that performs the following task:

- take two values from the main program:
  - the total of a number of values
  - the number of elements that make up the total
- calculate the average from the given values
- if the value is more than 60, return the word 'Accept'
- if not, return the word 'Reject'.

You must use **either**:

- OCR Exam Reference Language, or
- a high level language that you have studied. **[5]**

3 Create an algorithm that will use the function `averageValue()` from **Question 3**, assign the result to an appropriately named variable, and output the result.

You must use **either**:

- OCR Exam Reference Language, or
- a high level language that you have studied. **[3]**

4 Write pseudocode to:

A. assign a random integer between −5 and +25 inclusive to the variable `whole`

B. assign a random real number between 0.3 and 9.7 inclusive to the variable `number`. **[2]**

EXAM TIP 

Practice generating random numbers in your programs for different ranges of values.

Knowledge

28 Safe and readable programs

Avoid problems

Programmers must make sure their programs work, and produce the correct outputs.

However, there are other ways that programs can go wrong:

- they might be used by the wrong people
- user might enter bad inputs
- the code might be hard to read and understand.

Authentication

Many programs include **authentication**. Authentication checks user identity.

The purpose of authentication is to stop the wrong people from using a program. For example. hackers who try to steal money.

One method of authentication is for each user to input:

- a unique username
- the correct password for that username.

There may be a list of valid users and passwords. The program may search for the correct values by looking through the list.

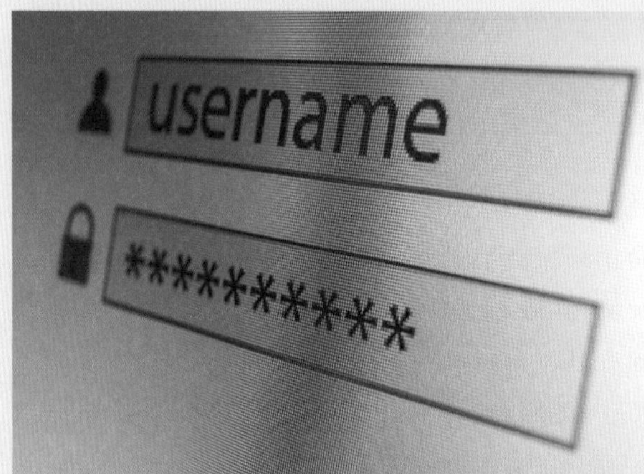

▲ ***Figure 1*** *Many programs require you to enter a username and password*

REVISION TIP

Consider how you use this type of authentication in your daily life and what information it is protecting.

LINK

Find out more in Chapter 31 Search algorithms.

Authentication example

The following program checks that both the user name and the password are correct. If they are not correct a procedure called quit() is called, which closes the program.

```
username = input("enter user name:")
password = input("enter password:")
if username == "admin" AND password == "abc123" then
   print("continue")
else
   quit()
endif
```

The username or password might be checked against a list saved in storage.

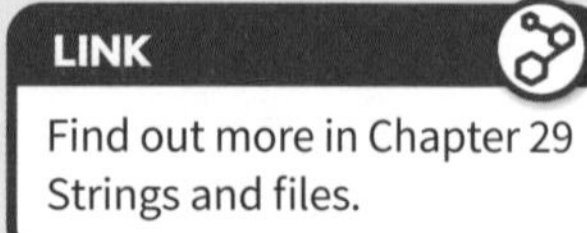

LINK

Find out more in Chapter 29 Strings and files.

Invalid inputs

Most programs get input from the user, but sometimes the input is bad.

Bad input from the user can make the program go wrong. This might mean:

- the program crashes
- the program runs but gives the wrong answer.

Experienced programmers design the program to avoid bad inputs. They test the program with a range of inputs to make sure it works in all cases.

One way to avoid bad inputs is to make your program **user-friendly**.

A user-friendly program is designed to be just that – easy to use. A user-friendly program has clear messages and prompts that will help the user to input the right values.

LINK 

Find out more in Chapter 24 Testing.

REVISION TIP 

A user-friendly program is easy for the users to understand.

Validation

Some errors will still occur, so programmers add **validation** to their programs.

Validation means checking inputs before they are used in the program, and stopping any bad inputs. For example, checking that inputs are:

- of the right data type
- in the right number range
- not left blank by mistake.

If the user input is wrong, the program shows an error message. The error message tells the user what the problem is. The bad input is not used. The user might get a second chance to input a value.

Make sure you can write a definition for these key terms.

authentication comment readable user-friendly validation

28 Safe and readable programs

Invalid input and validation example

This program divides a bonus of £1000 between the members of a team.

```
bonus = 1000
team = input("how many in the team?")
team = int(team)
pay = bonus/team
print(pay)
```

This line divides the bonus amount by the input value.

This program will crash if the user inputs the value 0. That is because the program divides by the input value. Dividing by zero causes a run-time error.

To prevent this error, the programmer added a validation check. The new code is shown in bold.

```
bonus = 1000
team = input("how many in the team?")
team = int(team)
while team == 0:
    team = input("Invalid data zero. Please re-enter")
    team = int(team)
endwhile
pay = bonus/team
print(pay)
```

If the user enters 0 the program will loop. The user will see an error message. The program will loop until the user enters a number that is not 0.

LINK 

Find out more in Chapter 22 Iteration (loop structures).

Readability

It is important to make sure your code is **readable**. Readable programs are easier for other programmers to understand.

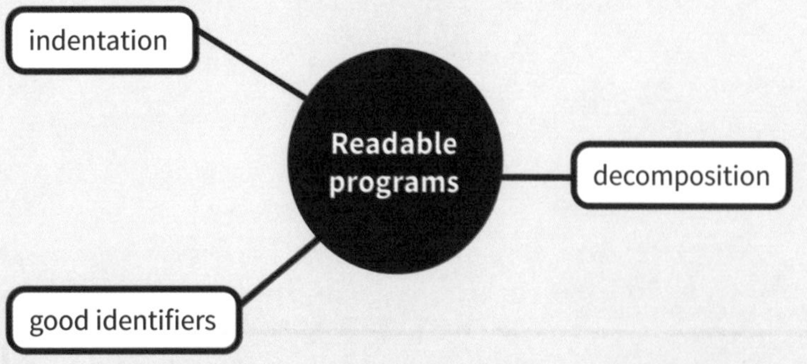

REVISION TIP 

A readable program is easy for other programmers to understand.

LINK 

Find out more in Chapter 18 Values and variables, Chapter 21 Selection structure, and Chapter 26 Decomposition.

Readability makes a program maintainable. It is easier to fix errors and add new features to the program.

Comments

One way to make your programs more readable is to add **comments**.

Comments are words in your program that are ignored by the computer. Comments are there to help the human reader and explain the code.

The code you see in the exam might include comments. Each comment begins with a // symbol. When the computer sees that symbol it ignores the rest of the line.

Here is an example of code that includes a comment.

```
// correct password is power123
password = input("enter the password:")
if password == "power123" then
   print("correct")
endif
```

This line is a comment.

Different programming languages use different symbols for comments.

Retrieval

Learn the answers to the questions below, then cover the answers column with a piece of paper and write down as many answers as you can. Check and repeat.

	Questions	Answers
1	What is the term for checking user identity in a program (for example with a password)	checking user identity is called authentication
2	Why should a program include checks on user identity?	the purpose of authentication is to stop the wrong people from using a program
3	How does user-friendly programming help to avoid bad inputs from the user?	user-friendly programming makes the program easier to use; prompts and messages to the user help them to input the correct values
4	What is the meaning of the term validation?	validation means checking inputs before they are used in the program, and stopping any bad inputs
5	What can be the result of bad user input?	bad user input can cause the program to crash; or the program runs but produces the wrong results
6	What should happen if the user enters bad input?	the input is blocked; an error message appears; the user may be able to try again
7	What does 'readable' programming mean?	readable programs can be easily read and understood by other programmers
8	List four features that make programs more readable	indentation; good identifiers; decomposition; comments
9	How is a comment different from other lines of code in a program?	the computer does not read the comments in a program
10	What is the purpose of comments in a program?	comments are there for other programmers to read; they explain the code

Put paper here

Previous questions

Now go back and use the questions below to check your knowledge from previous chapters.

	Previous questions	Answers
1	What is the difference between a procedure and a function?	a function returns a value, a procedure does not
2	If a variable is defined inside a procedure or function, where can it be used? What is the name of this type of variable?	if a variable is defined inside a sub program, it can only be used inside that sub program; it is called a local variable
3	Some commands are included inside a while loop. The test at the top of the loop is false. How many more times will these commands be carried out?	if the test at the top of the while loop is false, the commands inside the loop will not be carried out at all
4	A selection structure can include the keyword 'else'. Explain how the keyword 'else' controls the flow of a program.	commands that follow the keyword 'else' are carried out if the logical test is false
5	Write the final line of the code to define a procedure.	`endprocedure`

Put paper here

Practice

Exam-style questions

1 Explain how authentication can be applied by a program to confirm a user's identity. **[3]**

2 Create an algorithm to:

- input a number
- repeat until the number input is between 1 and 500 inclusive
- provide appropriate messages to the user at each stage
- Include comments.

You must use **either**:

- OCR Exam Reference Language, or
- a high level language that you have studied. **[5]**

EXAM TIP 

Remember the different types of loops available in your programming language or the OCR Exam Reference Language. Implement the most efficient type in your algorithm to suit the problem you are solving.

3 Explain why commenting is useful when designing algorithms. **[3]**

EXAM TIP 

Name other techniques that can be applied to make a program maintainable.

29 Strings and files

Strings and characters

A string is a data type. Values of the string data type are made of text characters. String values are enclosed in quotation marks. Strings cannot be used in calculations. A character is a string of length 1.

There are predefined functions and operators that can be used with strings. These functions and operators transform strings, creating new values.

LINK

Find out more in Chapter 18 Values and variables.

REVISION TIP

You will need to understand how to manipulate strings.

Predefined functions - ASCII values

Functions take parameter values and return new values to the main program. There are two predefined functions which process character values. They convert between text characters and ASCII values.

LINK

Find out more in Chapter 9 File size.

Function	What it does	Example	Result
`ASC()`	The parameter is a character. The returned value is the ASCII code number for that character.	`ASC("A")`	`65`
`CHR()`	The parameter is an ASCII code number. The returned value is the character for that code number.	`CHR(65)`	`"A"`

▲ ***Figure 1** Predefined character functions*

String operator - Concatenation

Concatenation means joining strings together to make a new, longer string.

The + operator is used for concatenation.

- When the + operator is between two number values it adds them.
- When the + operator is between two strings it concatenates them.

The result is a longer string made of the two strings joined together.

```
mystring = "Hello" +"World"
```

The value of the mystring variable is `"Hello World"`.

String methods

There are some other predefined subroutines used with strings. These are called **methods**.

Methods work like functions but they are written in a slightly different way.

To use a string method:

1. write the name of the string
2. write a dot
3. write the name of the method.

Some string methods are shown in **Figure 2**.

The example string variable 'mystring' is used to show the effect of each method.

```
mystring = "Hello World"
```

Method	Returned value	Example	Result
`.length`	Returns the number of characters in the string	`mystring.length`	`10`
`.upper`	Returns the string converted to upper case	`mystring.upper`	`"HELLO WORLD"`
`.lower`	Returns the string converted to lower case	`mystring.lower`	`"hello world"`

▲ ***Figure 2*** *Examples of string methods*

These methods create new values. They do not change the value of the original string. To use the value returned by a method, you need to assign it to a variable.

Slicing to make a substring

A **substring** is a new string. It is made by copying part of the original string.

The original string is not changed. A new, smaller string is returned.

Making a substring is also called **slicing** the string.

Method	Returned value	Example	Result
`.left(n)`	the leftmost n characters of the string	`mystring.left(5)`	`"Hello"`
`.right(n)`	the rightmost n characters of the string	`mystring.right(3)`	`"rld"`
`.substring(i,n)`	Start at character number i, count n characters	`mystring.substring(2,3)`	`"llo"`

▲ ***Figure 3*** *Substring methods*

The substring method uses a character number. That is the character where the substring begins. The numbering system begins at 0. The first character in the string is character 0, the next is character 1 and so on.

Knowledge

29 Strings and files

What are files?

Values in memory are lost when the program closes down. Sometimes you want to save values to use another time. That means using a file in storage.

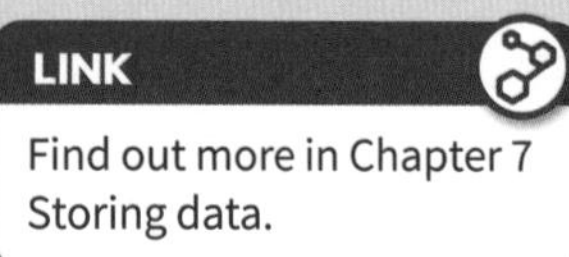

LINK
Find out more in Chapter 7 Storing data.

The main file operations are:

- **Write to:** Saving a value by copying it into a file in storage.
- **Read from:** Getting a value from a file in storage.

Before you read or write to a file, the file must be **opened**. After you have finished, the file must be **closed**.

Write to a file

In this example the file is called "password.txt". This program will open the file, write "hello" to the file, and then close the file.

```
myfile = newFile("password.txt")
myfile = open("password.txt")
myfile.writeLine("hello")
myfile.close()
```

This line makes a new file, if you want to use a file that already exists, you can leave out this line.

The new text "hello" will be added to the end of the file. You can use any other text you wish.

Read from a file

This example uses the same file. The program opens the file, reads the first line, and prints it out.

```
myfile = open("password.txt")
mystring = myfile.readLine()
print(mystring)
myfile.close()
```

Enter the file name here.

REVISION TIP 

Revise the structure of the command. The file name will be provided as part of the exam question.

Read every line

This example uses the same file. This program includes a loop.

The program opens the file, reads every line, and prints out each one.

```
myfile = open("password.txt")
while not myfile.endOfFile()
      mystring = myfile.readLine()
      print(mystring)
endwhile
myfile.close()
```

Loops until it reaches the end of the file.

Make sure you can write a definition for these key terms.

concatenation closed file method open file read from slicing substring write to

Retrieval

Learn the answers to the questions below, then cover the answers column with a piece of paper and write down as many answers as you can. Check and repeat.

	Questions	Answers
1	Strings can be concatenated. What does concatenate mean?	concatenate means joining strings together to make a bigger string
2	Describe the two functions used to convert between strings and ASCII values.	ASC(): given a character, returns the ASCII value; CHR(): given an integer, returns the character with that ASCII value
3	What value is returned by the string method `.length`?	the number of characters in the string
4	Describe the two methods used to convert a string to upper or lower case.	`string.upper` makes a string converted to upper case; `string.lower` makes a string converted to lower case
5	Slicing makes a new shorter string from a string value. What happens to the original string?	slicing does not change the original string. It just makes a new substring
6	What is the returned value of the command `mystring.left(5)`?	it returns a substring made out of the 5 characters on the left of mystring
7	What does it mean to read from a data file?	reading from a data file means getting a value from a file in storage
8	What does it mean to write to a data file?	writing to a data file means saving a value by copying it to a file in storage
9	What must you do with a file before you can read to or write to a file?	before you can read to or write to a file you must open the file
10	What must you do with a file after you have finished the read or write operation?	after you have read from or written to a file you must close the file

Put paper here

Previous questions

Now go back and use the questions below to check your knowledge from previous chapters.

	Previous questions	Answers
1	How does user-friendly programming help to avoid bad inputs from the user?	user-friendly programming makes the program easier to use; prompts and messages to the user help them to input the correct values
2	What is the meaning of the term validation?	validation means checking inputs before they are used in the program, and stopping any bad inputs
3	A sub program is called from the main program. How is the value of the parameter given in the main program?	the value of the parameter is given in brackets after the name of the sub program in the main program
4	Programs should be tested by running the program on a computer. But algorithms are not tested in this way. Why not?	algorithms are not written in a programming language; they cannot be run on a computer
5	How is a procedure called in the main program?	by writing the name of the procedure followed by opening and closing brackets

Put paper here

Exam-style questions

1 The ASCII code number for the letter `'A'` is 65, and for the letter `'a'`, it is 97.

Write the pseudocode to input any single uppercase letter then output its lowercase equivalent using the `ASC()` and `CHR()` functions. **[3]**

> **EXAM TIP**
> You don't need to memorise ASCII codes. If any are needed, they will be given in the question.

2 The string `"Computer Science is Fun"` is stored in the variable `myText`.

Complete the table by giving the output of each statement.

Statement	Output
`myText.right(3)`	
`myText.upper`	
`myText.left(4)`	
`myText.lower`	
`myText.length`	
`myText.substring(9,3)`	

[6]

3 Create an algorithm to:

- open a text file named `"books.txt"`
- read every line of the text file until the end of the file has been reached
- output each line of the file after it has been read.

You must use **either**:

- OCR Exam Reference Language, or
- a high level language that you have studied. **[5]**

4 Create an algorithm to:

- input a first name and a last name as strings
- concatenate the two strings into a single string with a space between them
- store the name into a new text file named `"contacts.txt"`.

You must use **either**:

- OCR Exam Reference Language, or
- a high level language that you have studied. **[5]**

> **EXAM TIP**
> When working with file handling, always remember to close the file at the end of your algorithm.

Knowledge

30 Arrays

What is an array?

A variable is a named storage location in computer memory. The storage location can hold a single data value.

An **array** is a data structure. Like a variable, an array has an identifier or name, but an array can store many data values.

To visualise an array, think of a series of boxes. Some of the boxes may be empty. Some of the boxes may hold data values.

In the example in **Figure 1**, the array has five storage locations.

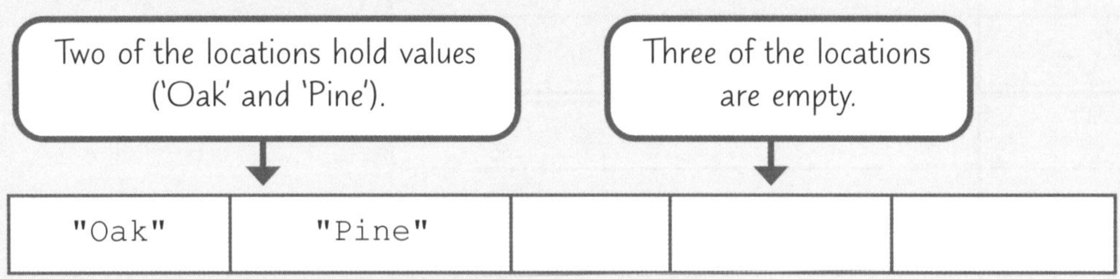
Two of the locations hold values ('Oak' and 'Pine').
Three of the locations are empty.
"Oak"
"Pine"

▲ ***Figure 1** An array is like a series of boxes*

LINK

Find out more in Chapter 18 Values and variables.

REVISION TIP

Some programming languages, such as Python, have a data type called a list. A list is different to an array. Lists are not fixed in size. Lists will not be mentioned in the exam.

Fixed in size

Before you can store values in an array, you need to make the array. The technical term is 'initialising' the array.

When you initialise an array, you must first set the size of the array. The command to create an array is:

```
array trees[5]
```

This command makes an array called trees. The array has five data locations. The number of locations is shown in square brackets.

When you make an array like this, the data locations are empty. Later commands might add values to the data locations. But the array will not change in size.

For this reason an array is called a **fixed length** data structure. The size is fixed when you make the array.

You can also make an array with the values already in place.

Here is an example.

```
array trees = ["Oak", "Pine", "Beech", "Holly", "Elm"]
```

The different values are shown in square brackets. They are separated by commas. All the values of an array must be the same data type.

Elements of an array

The data values in an array are called the **elements** of the array. Each element is given the name of the array, plus an **index number**.

This visualisation of an array shows the index numbers. The numbering starts at 0.

The number shows the location of the element in the array. It is called the index number.

0	1	2	3	4
"Oak"	"Pine"			

▲ ***Figure 2*** *Each element of an array has a number*

You can use the elements in programs. Give the name of the array, plus the index number in square brackets. For example:

```
trees[1]
```

This refers to the element with index number 1 in the array trees. The element can be used like any other variable in any program command. Here is an example. This command prints the element.

```
print(trees[1])
```

This command will print the data value 'Pine'.

Assign a value

You can assign a value to an element of an array. Assign a value as you would for any variable, using the equals sign. But remember to include an index number in square brackets. For example:

```
trees[3] = "Holly"
```

This command assigns the value 'Holly' to location 3. After this command the array would look like the array in **Figure 3**.

0	1	2	3	4
"Oak"	"Pine"		"Holly"	

▲ ***Figure 3*** *The value 'Holly' has been assigned to the array element with index number 3*

An array can have gaps and empty spaces in it. If you assign a value to a location that already has a value in it, the command will overwrite the old value.

In some programming languages, you are not allowed to leave empty spaces. In these cases the programmer might store a null value, or empty string, in the location. A null value is written as quote marks with nothing in between them like this:

```
""
```

30 Arrays

Traverse an array

Traversing an array means visiting every element in the array. For example, you could print out each element. A for loop (counter loop) is ideal for traversing an array.

Here is the code to traverse the array trees, and print out each element. The array has five elements in it, so the for loop must count from 0 to 4.

```
for i = 0 to 4
   print (trees[i])
next i
```

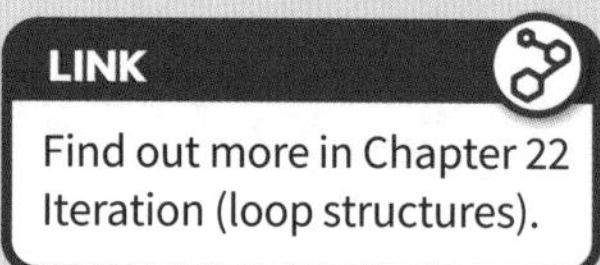

LINK

Find out more in Chapter 22 Iteration (loop structures).

1D and 2D arrays

The array trees is a **1D array**. A 1D array is a sequence of elements. Each element is identified by a single index number.

REVISION TIP

1D stands for one-dimensional. 2D stands for two-dimensional.

There are also **2D arrays**. A 2D array looks like a table, with rows and columns.

Figure 4 shows a visualisation of a 2D array. It has four rows and two columns. Remember: numbering starts at 0.

	0	1
0		
1		
2		
3		

▲ ***Figure 4*** *A 2D array*

To create an empty 2D array you must give two numbers. First the number of rows, then the number of columns. For example:

```
array animals[4,2]
```

Each data item in a 2D array is identified by two numbers – the row number, then the column number. For example, these commands assign values to individual data items:

```
animals[0,0] = "Cat"
animals[2,0] = "Dog"
```

1D and 2D arrays

After these commands the array will look like the one in **Figure 5**.

	0	1
0	"Cat"	
1		
2	"Dog"	
3		

▲ ***Figure 5*** *A 2D array containing the values "Cat" and "Dog"*

A 2D array can be used to store records in a data table.

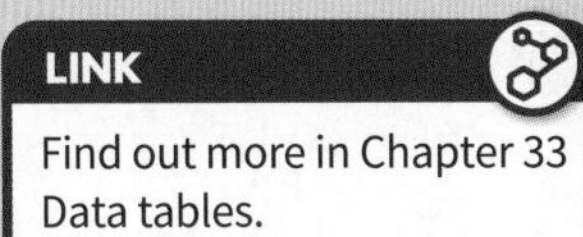

LINK

Find out more in Chapter 33 Data tables.

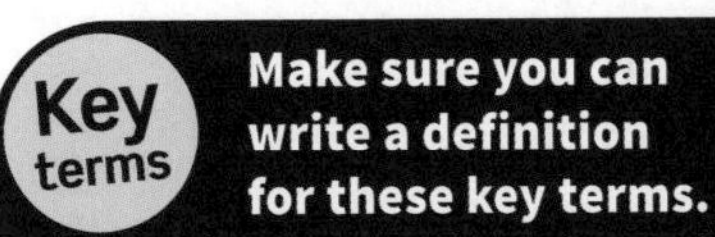

Key terms **Make sure you can write a definition for these key terms.**

1D 2D array elements fixed length index number

Retrieval

Learn the answers to the questions below, then cover the answers column with a piece of paper and write down as many answers as you can. Check and repeat.

	Questions	Answers
1	An array is an example of a data structure. What is a data structure?	a data structure holds a series of values, using a single identifier
2	An array is a fixed length data structure. What does 'fixed length' mean?	a fixed length data structure does not change in size when you add or remove values
3	When you create an empty array you must give the name of the array. What other information must you give?	the size of the array as a number in square brackets
4	You can create an array with data values in it. You must give the name of the array. What other information must you give?	give each of the data values separated by commas, in square brackets
5	All the elements of an array must be the same ... what?	all the elements of an array must be the same data type
6	How do you refer to a single element of a 1D array?	give the name of the array, then the index number in brackets
7	What number is given to the first element of an array?	0
8	Some arrays are 2D arrays. What does 2D mean?	two-dimensional
9	How can you visualise a 2D array, compared to a 1D array?	a 2D array can be visualised as a table of rows and columns
10	How do you refer to a single data item in a 2D array?	give two numbers: the row number, then the column number; the numbers are shown in square brackets, separated by a comma

Put paper here

Previous questions

	Previous questions	Answers
1	Strings can be concatenated. What does concatenate mean?	concatenate means joining strings together to make a bigger string
2	What value is returned by the string method `.length`?	the number of characters in the string
3	A function sends a value back to the main program. What command inside a function makes this happen?	the keyword 'return' followed by the value
4	List four features that make programs more readable	indentation; good identifiers; decomposition; comments
5	What is the term for checking user identity in a program (e.g. with a password)	checking user identity is called authentication

Put paper here

Exam-style questions

1 Explain what is meant by the phrase 'an array is a fixed length or static data structure'. **[2]**

2 Write the pseudocode to output the contents of a one-dimensional array with the identifier `stock`, which holds 50 elements. **[3]**

3 A two-dimensional array `contacts` is used to store the first names, last names, and telephone numbers of friends and family, organised as follows:

	0	1	2
0	*first name 1*	*last name 1*	*telephone number 1*
1	*first name 2*	*last name 2*	*telephone number 2*

The array has already been declared with 500 rows and three columns, and all the elements have been initialised with the null string `""`.

Create an algorithm to:

- find the first available free row in the array `contacts`
- input a first name, last name, and telephone number and store it in the first available free row.

You must use **either**:

- OCR Exam Reference Language, or
- a high level language that you have studied. **[5]**

EXAM TIP 

Some programming languages don't use arrays in the traditional way. If you have used one of those languages for your programming experience, you are advised to answer this type of question using the OCR Exam Reference Language.

Knowledge

31 Search algorithms

What is searching?

A data structure contains many data values. Searching means looking through a data structure for a particular value. The value is called a **search term**.

The result of a search can be True (the search term is found) or False (the search term is not in the data structure).

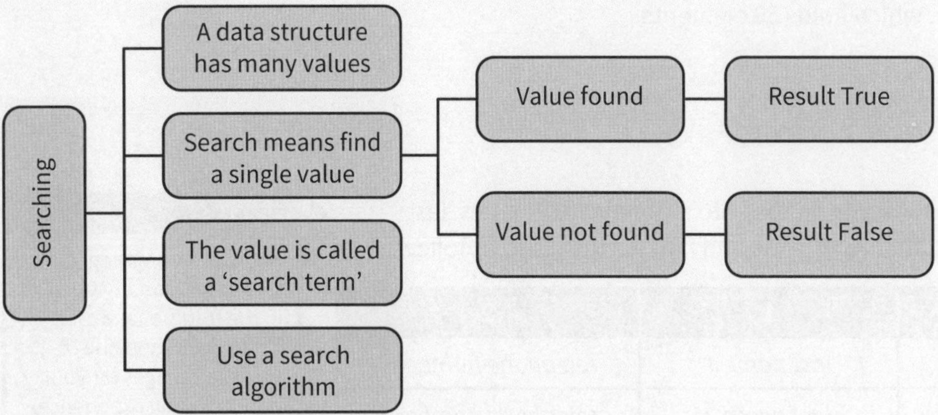

▲ ***Figure 1*** *Searching for a value in a data structure*

An algorithm is a series of steps to solve a problem.

There is more than one way to search for a value in a data structure. The different ways of searching are called **search algorithms**.

You need to know two search algorithms:

- **linear search**
- **binary search**.

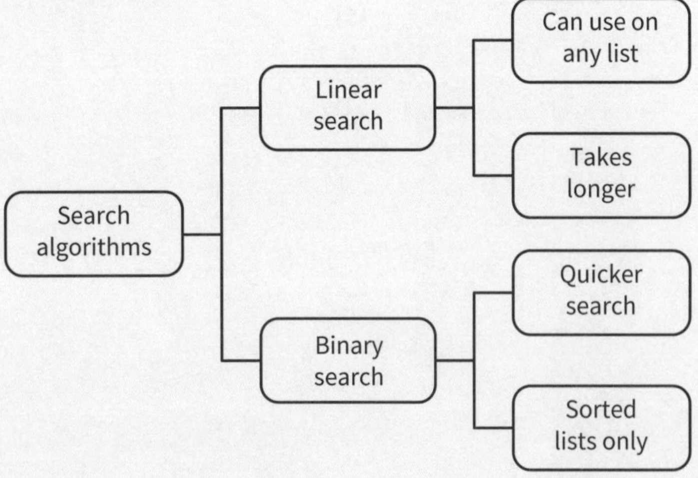

▲ ***Figure 2*** *Linear and binary search algorithms*

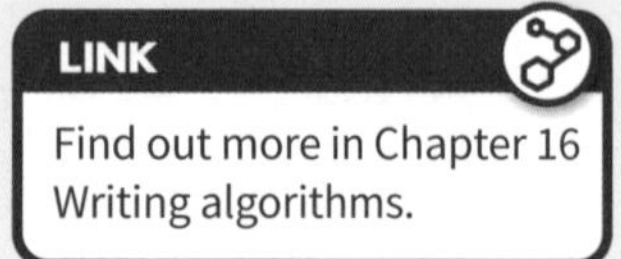

LINK

Find out more in Chapter 16 Writing algorithms.

Both of these algorithms will find a value in a linear data structure, such as a 1D array or array. The two algorithms work in different ways They have different benefits and limitations.

Linear search

A linear search:

- uses a for loop to traverse the array
- compares each item to the search term – if it matches, the item is found.

LINK

Find out more in Chapter 30 Arrays.

Here is the code for a linear search. This search will find the search term 'fox' in an array called animals. The array has 100 elements.

```
found = False
for i = 0 to 99
    if animals[i] == "fox" then
        found = True
    endif
next i
```

At the end of the linear search, the variable 'found' will have the value True (if the element was found) or False (if the element was not found).

Binary search

An alternative to the linear search is the binary search.

The binary search is a quicker way to find an item in an array. However, the binary search will only work if the array is sorted into numerical or alphabetical order.

LINK

Find out more in Chapter 32 Sort algorithms.

A binary search:

- finds the middle value in an array
- compares this middle value to the search term
    - if the term is bigger, slices the array in half and takes the upper half
    - If the term is smaller, slices the array in half and takes the lower half
- repeats these commands until there is an array of one element.

If this element matches the search term then it has been found. If this element does not match the search term then it is not in the array.

REVISION TIP

If the array has an even number of items there is no exact middle value. Use the item just below the middle as the midpoint.

Binary search code

This code is for a binary search.

This part of the algorithm splits the array in half and half again until it only has one element. It uses a while loop. The loop repeats while the array has more than one item in it.

LINK

Find out more in Chapter 22 Iteration (loop structures).

Knowledge

31 Search algorithms

Binary search code

```
while len(animals) > 1
   midpoint = len(array) DIV 2
   if array[midpoint] > "fox" then
         array = array[up to midpoint]
   else
         array = array[midpoint to end]
   endif
endwhile
```

Take the half of the array up to the midpoint.

Take the half of the array from the midpoint to the end.

This part of the algorithm compares the one remaining element to the search term.

```
if animals[0] == "fox" then
   found = True
else
   found = False
endif
```

REVISION TIP 

You do not need to learn the code for each of the search algorithms. However, you should be able to recognise the code, and you should be able to explain how each search algorithm finds a value in a 1D array.

REVISION TIP

Remember, binary search will only work if the array is sorted. A sorted array is a **pre-requisite** of the binary search algorithm.

Worked example

Show how a binary search would find the value 3 in the following array.

`[1,3,7,8,9]` — The search term is 3. The middle value of the array is 7. The middle value is larger than the search term. So slice the array in half, and take the lower half.

`[1,3]` — The array has an even number of elements. Round down, and take 1 as the midpoint. This is smaller than the search term, so we take the upper half of the array.

`[3]` — The array now has a single value in it. This matches the search term, so the value has been found.

Compare the searches

A linear search is slower than a binary search.

The linear search must loop through every item in the array to find the value. The binary search splits the array in half each time. That means it takes fewer steps to find the item.

Algorithm	Description	Advantages	Limitations
Linear search	A for loop counts through the array. Each item is compared to the search term.	Can be used with any array	Takes more steps – a slower search
Binary search	Splits the array in half and half again until the array has only one item. This item is compared to the search term.	Takes fewer steps – a faster search	Can only be used with a sorted array

▲ ***Figure 3*** *Advantages and disadvantages of linear and binary searches*

Search functions

The code for either search algorithm can be turned into a search function.

- The search term is passed as a parameter.
- The function returns True (if the search term was found) or False (if the search term is not in the array).

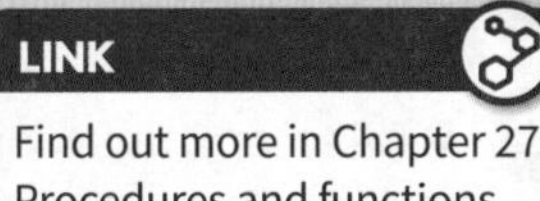

LINK

Find out more in Chapter 27 Procedures and functions.

Key terms **Make sure you can write a definition for these key terms.**

binary search linear search pre-requisite search algorithms search term

Retrieval

Learn the answers to the questions below, then cover the answers column with a piece of paper and write down as many answers as you can. Check and repeat.

	Questions	Answers
1	What is the purpose of a search algorithm?	a search algorithm is used to find an item in a linear data structure (such as a 1D array)
2	A search algorithm may be made into a function. What values should be returned?	a search function should return the values True or False
3	What is a search term?	a search term is the value that the search algorithm looks for in the array
4	What type of loop is used by a linear search algorithm?	a linear search algorithm uses a for loop that counts through every item in the array
5	How does the linear search algorithm work?	each item in the array is compared to the search term; if there is a match then the term is found; if the loop ends with no match, then the term is not in the array
6	Name one advantage of a linear search algorithm and one advantage of a binary search algorithm.	a linear search can be carried out on any array, whether or not it is sorted ; a binary search is completed in fewer steps, so the algorithm is quicker
7	What type of loop is used in a binary search algorithm?	a while loop is used in a binary search algorithm
8	What stops this loop?	it repeats until the array has one item in it
9	The binary search algorithm splits the array in half at the midpoint. Does it take the upper or lower half?	the value at the midpoint is compared to the search term; if the search term is smaller than the midpoint, take the lower half; if it is larger, take the upper half
10	At the end of the binary search you have an array with one value in it. What is the final stage of the binary search?	compare the one value that is left to the search term; if it matches, the value is found; if it does not match, the value is not in the array

Put paper here

Previous questions

Now go back and use the questions below to check your knowledge from previous chapters.

	Previous questions	Answers
1	An array is a fixed length data structure. What does 'fixed length' mean?	a fixed length data structure does not change in size when you add or remove values
2	When you create an empty array you must give the name of the array. What other information must you give?	the size of the array as a number in square brackets
3	Slicing makes a new shorter string from a string value. What happens to the original string?	slicing does not change the original string; it just makes a new substring
4	What are the disadvantages of using global variables?	global variables are risky; they can overwrite values in the program, causing unwanted side effects

Put paper here

Exam-style questions

1 Identify **one** requirement in the data for a binary search to function correctly. **[1]**

2 An array contains a list of numbers:

2, 12, 15, 16, 20, 22, 23, 25, 27, 28, 30, 35

Outline the steps used by a binary search to find the number 25 in the given list. **[4]**

3 Describe the steps a linear search would follow when searching for a specific name in a list of names. **[3]**

EXAM TIP

You do not need to learn the code for each of the search algorithms.

EXAM TIP

You should be able to recognise the code, and you should be able to explain how each search algorithm finds a value in a 1D array.

32 Sort algorithms

What is sorting?

An array is a 1D data structure that can hold many values.

All the values in an array are the same data type. The values in an array can be **sorted** into numerical or alphabetical order. Or they can be unsorted.

It can be useful to have a sorted instead of an unsorted array.

For example, the binary search is a fast way to search for a value, but it only works on a sorted array.

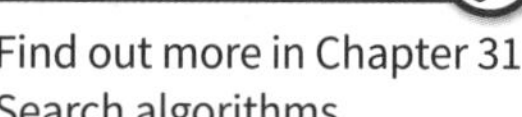
Find out more in Chapter 31 Search algorithms.

There is more than one way to sort an array. The different ways of sorting are called **sort algorithms**.

You need to know three sort algorithms:

- **bubble sort**
- **insertion sort**
- **merge sort**.

Overview of the sort algorithms

Figure 1 has the key facts you should learn about each algorithm.

Sort algorithm	How it works	Recognise the code	Discuss its use
Bubble	Traverse the array with a for loop. Swap values that are the wrong way round. Repeat until there are no more swaps.	A for loop inside a while loop	The slowest of the sort algorithms – only use with very short arrays
Insertion	Traverse the array. Pass any items that are out of place backwards to their correct position.	A for loop going forwards, then a for loop going backwards	Can be slow – but works fast if the array is already partly sorted
Merge	Split the array into single items. Merge them to make larger and larger arrays until all the items are in a single array.	Requires two functions *(you do not need to learn this code for the exam)*	This sort always works quickly. It is suitable to use with large and highly disordered arrays.

▲ ***Figure 1*** *The key facts for each sort algorithm*

REVISION TIP

You *do not need to learn to write sort algorithms in code*. You should be able to explain how each search algorithm works in general terms.

REVISION TIP

You should recognise the code for the bubble sort or insertion sort if it is shown in the exam.

Swapping values

Many sort algorithms depend on swapping values within an array. The code to swap values varies between different programming languages.

For example:

```
temp = a
a = b
b = temp
```

- `temp = a` ← Store the value in a in a variable called 'temp'.
- `a = b` ← Overwrite the value in a with the value in b.
- `b = temp` ← Overwrite the value in b with the value in temp.

It is common for programmers to call the variable 'temp'. This is because it is temporary storage for value in a during the swap. The variable will not be used anywhere else in the program.

In the examples in this chapter, we have written the code to swap two values like this.

```
swap(a,b)
```

REVISION TIP 

Remember! There is always more than one way to write any algorithm, and the details will vary between different programming languages.

Bubble sort code

Here is a bubble sort algorithm written using pseudocode.

In this example the array is called animals and has 100 items.

```
while swaps == true
    swaps = false
    for i = 0 to 98
        if animals[i] > animals[i+1]
            swap(animals[i], animals[i+1])
            swaps = true
        endif
    next i
endwhile
```

`for i = 0 to 98` ← The for loop does not count to the very end of the array (100 items numbered 0 to 99). Instead it counts to one less than the length of the array (99 items numbered 0 to 98).

`swap(animals[i], animals[i+1])` ← If the for loop counted from 0 to 99, there would be a run-time error at this line, because 99 + 1 = 100 and animals[100] doesn't exist.

Notice the typical structure of a bubble sort algorithm: a for loop inside a while loop.

Knowledge

32 Sort algorithms

Insertion sort code

Here is the insertion sort algorithm written using pseudocode. This example sorts an array called animals, of length 100.

```
for i = 0 to 98
   for x = i+1 to 1 step -1
         if animals[x] < animals[x-1] then
               swap(animals[x], animals[x-1])
         endif
   next x
next i
```

Notice the typical structure of the insertion sort algorithm: two for loops, one going forwards from 0 to 99, the next going backwards to 0 in steps of minus one. The two for loops use different counter variables. The first counter variable in this example is i, the second counter variable is x.

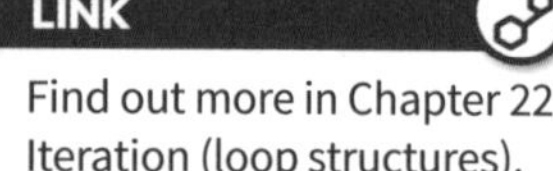

LINK
Find out more in Chapter 22 Iteration (loop structures).

Merge sort

The merge sort is a fast and reliable sort that works quickly on any kind of array, even one that is disordered. The merge sort works by splitting an array into a group of small arrays, each with one item. These small arrays are then merged into arrays of length two, then length four and so on until you are left with one sorted array.

You will not have to write this code, but you should be able to show how the merge sort would work on an example array.

Worked example

Show, step by step, how a merge sort would sort the following array.

`[2,19,10,3]` — First the array is split to make four arrays of only one item.

`[2] [19] [10] [3]` — Then these are merged to make arrays of 2.

`[2, 19] [3, 10]` — Then these arrays are merged in turn to make arrays of 4.

`[2, 3, 10, 19]` — The process continues until there is one large array, in sorted order.

Sort functions

The code to sort an array can be turned into a sort function.

- The function takes an unsorted array as a parameter.
- The function returns a sorted array.

The details of how arrays can be passed and returned by functions will vary between programming languages. Many programming languages include a predefined sort function.

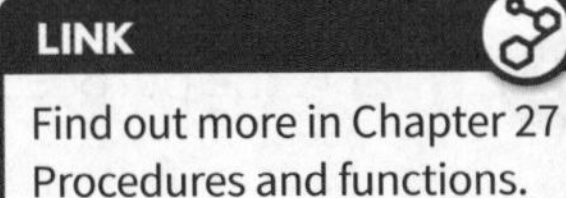

LINK
Find out more in Chapter 27 Procedures and functions.

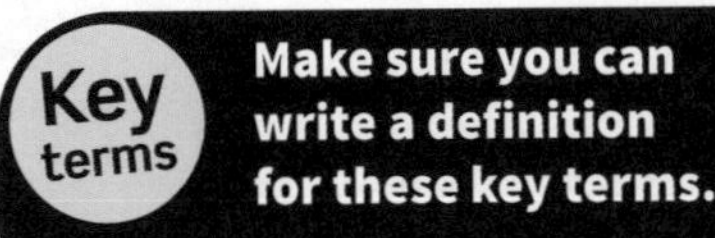

Key terms **Make sure you can write a definition for these key terms.**

bubble sort   insertion sort   merge sort   sort algorithm   sorted array

Retrieval

Learn the answers to the questions below, then cover the answers column with a piece of paper and write down as many answers as you can. Check and repeat.

	Questions	Answers
1	What is the purpose of a sort algorithm?	a sort algorithm puts an array into numerical or alphabetical order
2	Which sort algorithm uses a for loop inside a while loop?	a bubble sort algorithm
3	Which sort algorithm uses a backwards for loop inside a forwards for loop?	a insertion sort algorithm
4	Which sort algorithm starts by splitting the array into small arrays with only one item in each array?	a merge sort algorithm
5	What does the sort algorithm from **question 4** do after the array has been split into single items?	the arrays are merged and merged again until there is one large sorted array
6	Which is generally considered to be the slowest sort algorithm?	a bubble sort
7	Which type of array is the insertion sort is a good choice for?	an array that is already partially sorted
8	Which search algorithm is fastest for sorting a large and very disordered array?	a merge sort
9	Give a brief overview of how an insertion sort works.	traverse the array once using a for loop; any items that are out of place are passed backwards to their correct position
10	Give a brief overview of how the bubble sort works.	traverse the array with a for loop; swap any values that are the wrong way round; repeat the traversal until there are no more swaps

Put paper here

Previous questions

Now go back and use the questions below to check your knowledge from previous chapters.

	Previous questions	Answers
1	What is a search term?	a search term is the value that the search algorithm looks for in the array
2	What type of loop is used by a linear search algorithm?	a linear search algorithm uses a for loop that counts through every item in the array
3	What number is given to the first element of an array?	0
4	What does it mean to write to a data file?	writing to a data file means saving a value by copying it to a file in storage
5	How is a comment different from other lines of code in a program?	the computer does not read the comments in a program

Put paper here

Exam-style questions

1 Identify the type of algorithm in the following pseudocode:

```
while swap == true
  swap = false
  for loop = 0 to 499
    if names[loop] > names[loop + 1]
      temp = names[loop]
      names[loop] = names[loop + 1]
      names[loop + 1] = temp
      swap = true
    endif
  next loop
endwhile
```

[1]

EXAM TIP

You do not need to remember the code for sort algorithms.

EXAM TIP

You should be able to explain how each sort algorithm works in general terms and recognise the code for the bubble sort or insertion sort.

2 Outline the main steps a bubble sort will follow to sort a set of names held in the array `names` into **descending** order. **[4]**

3 Describe the main steps an insertion sort will follow to sort a set of numbers in the array `payments` into **ascending** order. **[4]**

4 A program stores the following list of numbers sorted into **descending** order using a merge sort.

Complete the merge sort of the data by showing each step of the process.

1960	2020	1980	1963	2016	2009	2012	1957

[4]

EXAM TIP

You need to be able to apply any of the sort algorithms to a given data set.

EXAM TIP

Practice applying the data set in **question 4** to the bubble sort and insertion sort algorithms.

Knowledge

33 Data tables

What is a data table

A data **table** is a way of storing all the facts about a particular topic or subject.

REVISION TIP

Data means 'facts'.

For example, it could store the data about all the goods for sale in a business. If you need to store facts about more than one subject, then you need more than one data table.

A data table is made of rows and columns.

Figure 1 shows part of a simplified data table called 'goods'. It stores data about the goods for sale in a business.

One column stores a single type of fact – this is called a **field**.

Code	Description	Quantity	Price
0001	Gas boiler	25	1750
0002	Condenser	150	1200
0003	Thermostat	230	150
0004	Heat pump	50	5900
0005	Radiator	599	80
0006	Hydrogen boiler	15	2500

One row stores all the facts about one item – this is called a **record**.

▲ ***Figure 1*** *A data table called 'goods'*

The table in **Figure 1** has:

- six records
- four fields.

That means it stores four facts about six different items.

Storing data using a 2D array

You can create an empty data table as a 2D array.

Find out more in Chapter 30 Arrays.

For example, the goods table could be stored in an array with 6 rows and 4 columns:

```
array goods[6,4]
```

To create records, you can assign values to each row of the array. For example:

```
array goods[0] = ["0001","Gas boiler","25", "1750"]
```

You can refer to a single data item in the table using two numbers. For example, to print out the price of a radiator:

```
print(goods[4][3])
```

Storing data using a 2D array

There are several disadvantages to using a 2D array to make a data table:

- all the values in the array must be the same data type
- to pick out a value you must know the correct row and column number.

For these reasons it can be more convenient to store data using a database of records.

Storing data using records

A data table is made of records (the rows) and fields (the columns).

- To define a data table you must give the name and data type of all the fields in the table.
- Each record in the table will be made of the same fields.

Storing data using records and fields has many advantages compared to using a 2D array.

- The fields can be different data types.
- You can use field names instead of needing to know the number of the field.
- Programming commands make it easy to find and display data values.

A collection of related data tables is called a **database**. There are programming languages that let you define and work with a database. The most widely used database language is **SQL**.

What is SQL

SQL stands for structured query language. SQL is a specialist programming language used to work with databases. It lets you create tables made of records and fields. It allows you to find and display data from the data tables in the database.

REVISION TIP 

If you have to write SQL you will be shown a data table.

REVISION TIP 

Pay careful attention to the names of any fields, and the name of the table. You will need to use these names in your SQL command.

How to write SQL

SQL keywords can be written in upper or lower case. Many programmers use upper case to make the keywords stand out. You can write the keywords on the same line or on different lines. The code will still work.

REVISION TIP 

Learn three SQL keywords:

- **SELECT**
- **FROM**
- **WHERE**

33 Data tables

SELECT... FROM ...

Using SQL you can select which fields you want to see.

- Write the keyword **SELECT** followed by the names of the fields, separated by commas.
- Write the keyword **FROM** followed by the name of the data table.

For example:

```
SELECT description, price
FROM goods
```

This command would show the description and price fields from the table called goods. The output of the command would look like this.

```
Gas boiler          1750
Condenser           1200
Thermostat          150
Heat pump           5900
Radiator            80
Hydrogen boiler     2500
```

SELECT... FROM... WHERE

Often you want to pick out individual records from the data table.

To do this use the key word **WHERE**, followed by a **search condition**. For example:

```
SELECT description, price
FROM goods
WHERE description = "Radiator"
```

This command will find the record where the description field contains the value 'Radiator'.

```
Radiator     80
```

To make the search condition you use comparison operators.

SELECT... FROM... WHERE

Some key comparison operators used in SQL are shown in **Figure 2**.

Operator	Meaning
=	Equal to
<>	Not equal to
<	less than
>	greater than

▲ ***Figure 2*** *SQL comparison operators*

REVISION TIP 

SQL operators are similar but not identical to the operators used in Exam Reference Language.

LINK 

Find out more in Chapter 19 Operators.

Worked example

Write the SQL command to display the code and description of all the items in the goods table that have a quantity greater than 100.

```
SELECT code, description
```

First use the key word SELECT followed by the names of the fields. In this case the fields are code and description.

```
SELECT code, description
FROM goods
```

Then use the key word FROM followed by the name of the table. In this case the table is called goods.

```
SELECT code, description
FROM goods
WHERE quantity > 100
```

Then finally use a search condition to find the right records. In this case you need records where the quantity is greater than 100.

Make sure you can write a definition for these key terms.

database field record search condition
SELECT... FROM... WHERE SQL table

Retrieval

Learn the answers to the questions below, then cover the answers column with a piece of paper and write down as many answers as you can. Check and repeat.

	Questions	Answers
1	What do you call the part of a data table that stores all the facts about a single item?	a record
2	What do you call the part of a data table that stores a single type of fact?	a field
3	What type of array can be used to store a data table?	a 2D array
4	What are the disadvantages of using an array to store a data table?	all the items in an array must be the same data type; the values in the array are referred to using two index numbers
5	What does SQL stand for?	structured query language
6	What is SQL used for?	SQL is a specialist language used to work with databases
7	What SQL keyword is used to pick out individual fields from a data table? Explain how it is used.	the keyword SELECT is used to pick out individual fields from a data table; write the word SELECT then the names of the fields, separated by commas
8	What SQL keyword is used to give the name of the data table? Explain how it is used.	the keyword FROM is used to identify the data table; write the word FROM then the name of the table
9	What SQL key word is used to state a search condition? Explain how it is used.	the keyword WHERE is used to state a search condition; write the word WHERE then give a search condition using an operator
10	Give four operators that can be used in SQL search conditions, with their meanings.	= equal to <> not equal to < less than > greater than

Put paper here

Previous questions

Now go back and use the questions below to check your knowledge from previous chapters.

	Previous questions	Answers
1	Which is generally considered to be the slowest sort algorithm?	a bubble sort
2	Which sort algorithm uses a backwards for loop inside a forwards for loop?	a insertion sort algorithm
3	An array is an example of a data structure. What is a data structure?	a data structure holds a series of values, using a single identifier
4	What is an advantage of a binary search algorithm compared to a linear search algorithm?	a binary search is completed in fewer steps, so the algorithm is quicker
5	What should happen if the user enters bad input?	the input is blocked; an error message appears; the user may be able to try again

Put paper here

Exam-style questions

The following table represents a part of a stock database for a television shop. The table is called `TblStock`.

Code	ScreenSize	SmartTv	Oled	Connectors	Price
758652	75	True	True	5	£4985.00
652685	65	True	True	5	£3250.00
605832	60	True	True	4	£2950.00
602585	60	False	False	3	£2750.00
557625	55	True	True	5	£2750.00
556821	55	False	False	4	£2350.00
556782	55	False	False	3	£2100.00
509856	50	True	True	4	£1750.00
509765	50	True	False	3	£1,350.00
509685	50	False	False	3	£1,100.00
409874	40	True	False	3	£750.00
409872	40	False	False	2	£500.00

The data in this table is referenced in the following questions.

1 Explain how a two-dimensional array can be used to emulate a database table and store the data in the table `TblStock`. Assume all the data has already been converted to the same data type using casting. **[3]**

2 Write the output that would be given by the following SQL statement.

```
SELECT Code, ScreenSize
FROM TblStock
WHERE Connectors = 4
```

[3]

3 Write the SQL statement to display all the fields from `TblStock` where the television is a smart TV. **[4]**

EXAM TIP

If you have to write SQL in the exam you will be shown a data table. Pay careful attention to:

- the names of any fields
- the name of the table.

You will need to use these names in your SQL statement, and the spellings must be accurate.

Knowledge

34 Electronic logic

Logic inside the processor

The computer system carries out logical and mathematical operations.

The work is done inside the processor, by a component called the ALU. All the processing is done electronically.

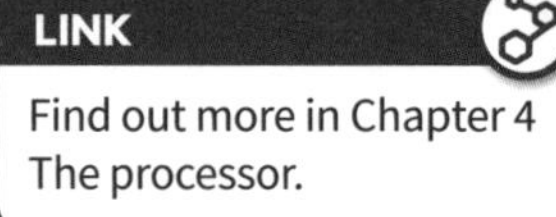

LINK

Find out more in Chapter 4 The processor.

Data inside the computer is represented as on/off electrical signals.

- An OFF signal is represented as a 0.
- An ON signal is represented as a 1.

Boolean expressions can be True or False.

- A True expression is represented by an ON signal, or the number 1.
- A False expression is represented by an OFF signal or the number 0.

Inputs and outputs

Programs tell the computer what processes to carry out. Program commands and operators transform inputs into outputs.

In the processor this is carried out by passing the electrical signals through circuits. The circuits change the electrical charge. They change the electrical charge in line with the laws of maths and logic.

This section is about the three Boolean operators: AND, OR, and NOT.

These operators:

- take Boolean expressions as input
- output new Boolean expressions.

The ALU changes inputs into outputs using special circuits called **logic gates**. There is a different gate for each operator.

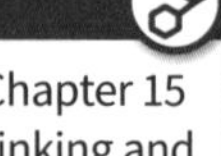

LINK

Find out more in Chapter 15 Computational thinking and Chapter 19 Operators.

NOT

The **NOT** operator reverses the value of a Boolean expression.

- If an expression is True it changes it to False.
- If an expression is False it changes it to True.

This is similar to how we use the word 'not' in everyday speech. Adding 'not' to a sentence changes the meaning of what we say.

This operation is carried out by an electronic circuit called a NOT gate.

The NOT gate is represented by the symbol shown in **Figure 1**.

The small circle at the point of the triangle is an important part of the symbol.

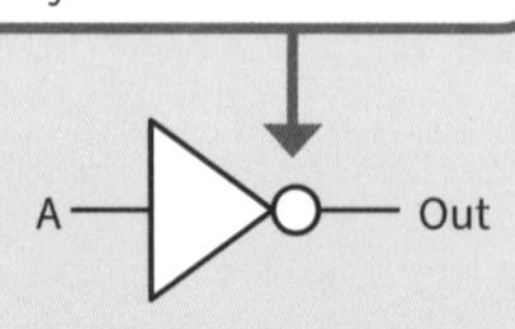

▲ ***Figure 1*** *A NOT gate*

NOT

The inputs to a logic gate are usually named after letters of the alphabet. The **NOT** gate has one input and one output. The gate changes the electrical signal.

The action of a NOT gate is summarised in **Figure 2**. 1 stands for an electrical signal. 0 stands for no electrical signal.

A	NOT A
0	1
1	0

▲ ***Figure 2*** *The action of a NOT gate*

This shows that the output of a NOT gate is always the reverse of the input. You can write the two values as 'True' and 'False' or as the numbers 1 and 0. A table like this, that summarises the inputs and outputs of a gate, is called a **truth table**.

AND

The **AND** operator joins two Boolean expressions to make a new Boolean expression. If both the parts of the expression are True, then the new expression is True. If either of the expressions is False, then the new expression is False. This is similar to the way we use the word 'and' in everyday speech.

This operation is carried out by an electronic circuit called an AND gate. It is flat at the back and rounded at the front.

An AND gate is shown in **Figure 3**.

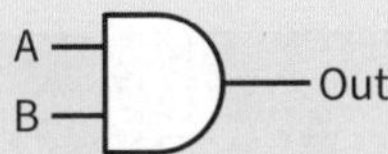

▲ ***Figure 3*** *An AND gate*

REVISION TIP 

Practice drawing the AND gate. It has a rounded front and a flat back.

The gate has two inputs (called A and B). It has one output. The action of the AND gate is summarised in the truth table in **Figure 4**. There are four possible combinations of A and B, so the table has four rows.

A	B	A AND B
0	0	0
0	1	0
1	0	0
1	1	1

▲ ***Figure 4*** *The action of an AND gate*

This shows that the output of the AND gate is always 0 (False) unless both A and B are set to 1.

34 Electronic logic

OR

The **OR** operator joins two Boolean expressions to make a new Boolean expression. If either part of the expression is True, then the whole expression is True. If both parts of the expressions are False, then the new expression is False. This is similar to the way we use the word 'or' in everyday speech.

This operation is carried out by an electronic circuit called an OR gate. It is rounded at the back and pointed at the front.

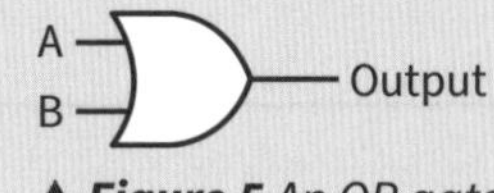

▲ ***Figure 5*** *An OR gate*

An OR gate is shown in **Figure 5**.

The gate has two inputs. It has one output. The action of the OR gate is summarised in the truth table in **Figure 6**. There are four possible combinations of A and B, so the table has four rows.

A	B	A OR B
0	0	0
0	1	1
1	0	1
1	1	1

▲ ***Figure 6*** *The action of an OR gate*

This shows that the output of the gate is always 1 (True) unless both A and B are set to 0.

Real-life logic

The computer can use logic gates to make real-life systems work. For example, to log on to a network a user must give a name and a password. Both conditions must be True. This matches the AND gate.

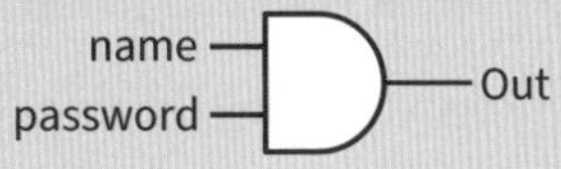

name
password
Out

▲ ***Figure 7*** *An AND gate for checking name and password*

name	password	log on to network
False	False	False
False	True	False
True	False	False
True	True	True

▲ ***Figure 8*** *Truth table for a name and password AND gate*

Make sure you can write a definition for these key terms.

AND logic gate NOT OR truth table

Retrieval

Learn the answers to the questions below, then cover the answers column with a piece of paper and write down as many answers as you can. Check and repeat.

Questions | Answers

1 What are the three Boolean operators

AND, OR, NOT

2 Describe in words the effect of the NOT operator.

the NOT operator reverses the value of a Boolean expression; if an expression is True it changes it to False; if an expression is False it changes it to True

3 Draw the NOT gate.

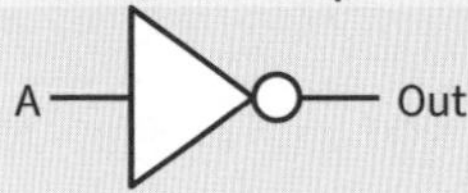

4 Draw the truth table of the NOT gate.

A	NOT A
0	1
1	0

5 Describe in words the effect of the AND operator.

the AND operator joins two Boolean expressions to make a new Boolean expression; if both the parts of the expression are True, then the new expression is True; if either or both of the expressions are False, then the new expression is False

6 Draw the AND gate.

7 Draw the truth table of the AND gate.

A	B	A AND B
0	0	0
0	1	0
1	0	0
1	1	1

8 Describe in words the effect of the OR operator.

the OR operator joins two Boolean expressions to make a new Boolean expression; if any part of the expression is True, then the new expression is True; if both parts of the expressions are False, then the new expression is False

9 Draw the OR gate

A

B

Output

Put paper here

Previous questions

Now go back and use the questions below to check your knowledge from previous chapters.

Previous questions | Answers

1 What type of array can be used to store a data table?

a 2D array

2 A program includes a command to convert an input string of letters to the integer data type. What type of error is this?

a command to convert a value to the wrong data type is an example of a run-time error

3 What is an advantage of a linear search algorithm compared to a binary search algorithm?

a linear search can be carried out on any array, whether or not it is sorted

Put paper here

Practice

Exam-style questions

1 Draw the logic gate symbols for an AND gate **and** an OR gate.

AND

OR **[2]**

2 Draw the truth tables for a NOT gate **and** an AND gate.

NOT

AND **[2]**

EXAM TIP

You need to memorise the symbols and truth tables for the AND, OR, and NOT gates.

3 Outline the effect the following logic gates have on their inputs:

- OR gate
- NOT gate. **[2]**

EXAM TIP

You will only be asked about AND, OR, and NOT gates.

35 Logic diagrams

Joining logic gates together

Logic gates can be joined together to make **logic circuits**.

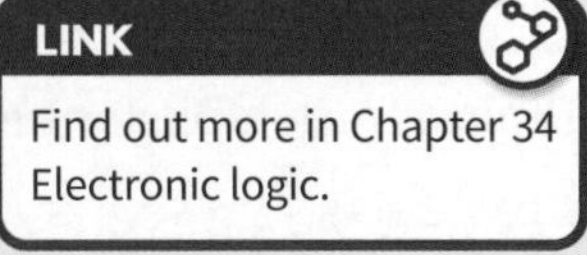

LINK

Find out more in Chapter 34 Electronic logic.

The electrical output of one gate is wired to make the electrical input to the next gate. A drawing that shows how the gates are wired together is called a **logic diagram.**

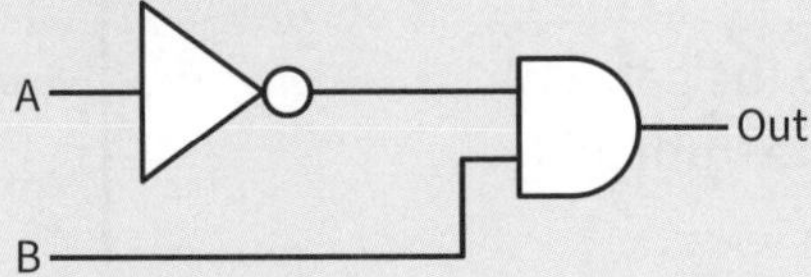

▲ ***Figure 1*** *A logic diagram*

The logic circuit in **Figure 1** has two inputs, A and B. There are four possible combinations of A and B.

A	B	output
0	0	
0	1	
1	0	
1	1	

▲ ***Figure 2*** *Incomplete truth table for the logic diagram in **Figure 1***

These are the inputs to the circuit. However, you also need to understand what the outputs of the circuit are.

Draw a truth table from a logic diagram

To find the output of a logic circuit you will need to draw a truth table.

The final column of the truth table will show the output of the circuit.

Check each logic gate in turn → What are the inputs and outputs of the gate? → Write the outputs as a new column in the table

Knowledge

35 Logic diagrams

Draw a truth table from a logic diagram

Worked example

Draw a truth table for the logic diagram in **Figure 1**.

Review the gates one at a time.

A	B	NOT A
0	0	1
0	1	1
1	0	0
1	1	0

The first gate is a NOT gate. The input to the gate is A. The output is NOT A. Add a column to the truth table. In this column show NOT A.

A	B	NOT A	NOT A AND B
0	0	1	0
0	1	1	1
1	0	0	0
1	1	0	0

The next gate is an AND gate. The inputs to the gate are NOT A and B. The output will be True if both the inputs are True. Fill in the final column.

This completes the truth table. The final column shows the output of the whole circuit. The output is 1 only when A is 0 and B is 1.

Real-life logic

Logic circuits can be used to solve real-life logic problems.

For example, an art gallery installed a burglar alarm. The alarm is triggered if both of these things are true:

- the door to the gallery is opened

AND

- the right passcode is NOT entered.

Here is the logic diagram that matches the problem.

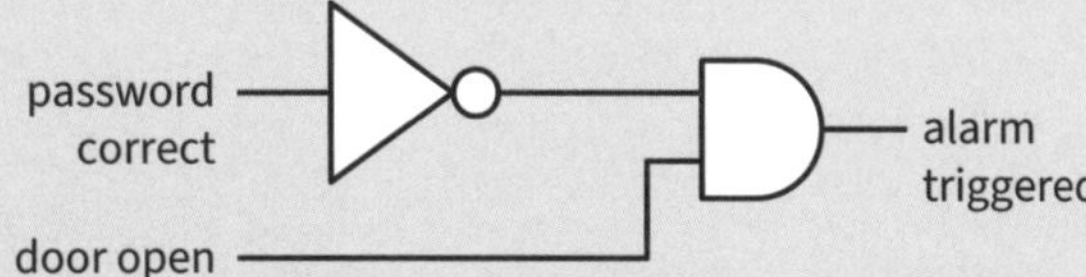

▲ ***Figure 3** A logic diagram for an art gallery alarm*

Real-life logic

The corresponding truth table in **Figure 4** sets out all possible combinations of input. Alarm triggered is True only when Door open is True and Passcode correct is False.

Door open	Passcode correct	NOT passcode correct	Alarm triggered
0	0	1	0
0	1	0	0
1	0	1	1
1	1	0	0

▲ ***Figure 4*** *Truth table for an art gallery alarm*

Circuits with three inputs

Some logic circuits have more than two inputs.

Three input values gives eight different possible combinations of input, as shown in the truth table in **Figure 6**.

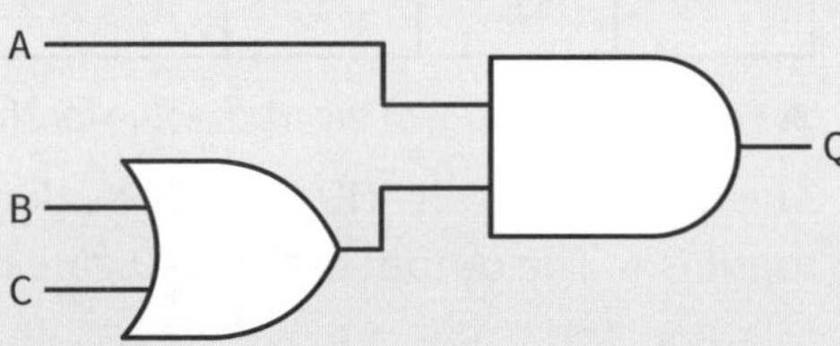

▲ ***Figure 5*** *The three inputs are usually labelled A, B and C*

A	B	C
0	0	0
0	0	1
0	1	0
0	1	1
1	0	0
1	0	1
1	1	0
1	1	1

▲ ***Figure 6*** *Truth table for a logic diagram with three inputs*

The eight combinations match the first eight binary numbers, from zero to seven.

000, 001, 010, 011, 100, 101, 110, 111

REVISION TIP 

If you know binary counting, this will help you remember the inputs to a three-value truth table.

LINK 

Find out more in Chapter 1 Binary numbers.

35 Logic diagrams

Draw a three-value truth table

A three-value truth table works in the same way as a two-value truth table. Add columns for each gate one at a time. **Figure 7** shows the first step of this process for the circuit in **Figure 5**. The first gate is B OR C. This value is 1 in every row where B is 1, or C is 1, or both.

A	B	C	B OR C
0	0	0	0
0	0	1	1
0	1	0	1
0	1	1	1
1	0	0	0
1	0	1	1
1	1	0	1
1	1	1	1

▲ ***Figure 7** First step in the truth table for the circuit in **Figure 5***

The final gate is an AND gate. The value (B OR C) goes into the AND gate. The other input is A. The output of the AND gate is 1 if both the inputs are 1.

Figure 8 shows the completed truth table.

A	B	C	B OR C	(B OR C) AND A
0	0	0	0	0
0	0	1	1	0
0	1	0	1	0
0	1	1	1	0
1	0	0	0	0
1	0	1	1	1
1	1	0	1	1
1	1	1	1	1

▲ ***Figure 8** Completed truth table for the circuit in **Figure 5***

The output of the final gate is the output of the whole circuit.

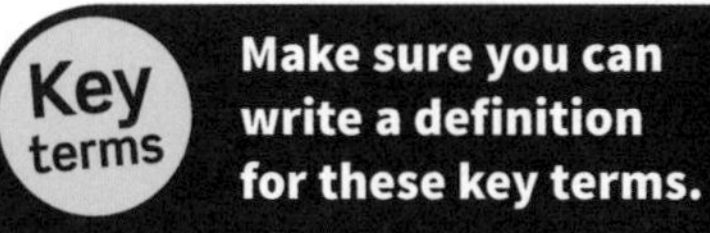
Key terms
Make sure you can write a definition for these key terms.

logic circuit   logic diagram

Retrieval

Learn the answers to the questions below, then cover the answers column with a piece of paper and write down as many answers as you can. Check and repeat.

	Questions	Answers
1	A logic circuit has two inputs, A and B. What are the possible combinations of input to the circuit?	a logic circuit with two inputs has four possible combinations of input: 00, 01, 10 and 11
2	A logic circuit has three inputs. How many possible combinations of input will there be?	a logic circuit with three inputs has eight possible combinations of input
3	A vending machine offers several ways to get a coffee. You can insert a token. You can press a button. You can press the button and insert a token. What logic gate matches the vending machine?	the OR gate
4	In question 3, what combination of inputs means you do NOT get a coffee?	if you do NOT insert a token AND you do NOT press the button
5	Questions 5 to 10 all refer to this diagram. What are the inputs to the AND gate? 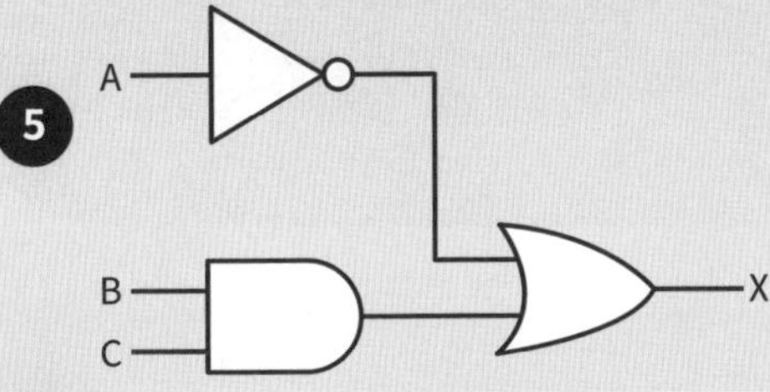	B and C
6	What is the input to the NOT gate?	A
7	When is the output of the AND gate 1?	when B is 1 and C is 1
8	When is the output of the NOT gate 1?	when A is 0
9	List the two inputs to the OR gate.	NOT A B AND C
10	Draw a truth table to match the whole circuit.	(see table below)

Put paper here

Answer to question 10:

A	B	C	NOT A	B AND C	OUTPUT
0	0	0	1	0	1
0	0	1	1	0	1
0	1	0	1	0	1
0	1	1	1	1	1
1	0	0	0	0	0
1	0	1	0	0	0
1	1	0	0	0	0
1	1	1	0	1	1

Retrieval

Previous questions

Now go back and use the questions below to check your knowledge from previous chapters.

	Previous questions	Answers
1	How is a comment different from other lines of code in a program?	the computer does not read the comments in a program
2	How does increasing cache size increase processor speed?	it is quicker for the processor to fetch instructions and data from cache memory; if the cache memory is larger, then more of the instructions and data can be stored in this fast-access memory
3	What is a software license?	an agreement that you can make use of software; it usually includes payment and lasts for a set time only

Put paper here

Practice

Exam-style questions

1 A logic system **X = (A AND B) OR (B AND NOT C)** is to be constructed.

Complete the following logic diagram for **X = (A AND B) OR (B AND NOT C)** by drawing one logic gate in each box.

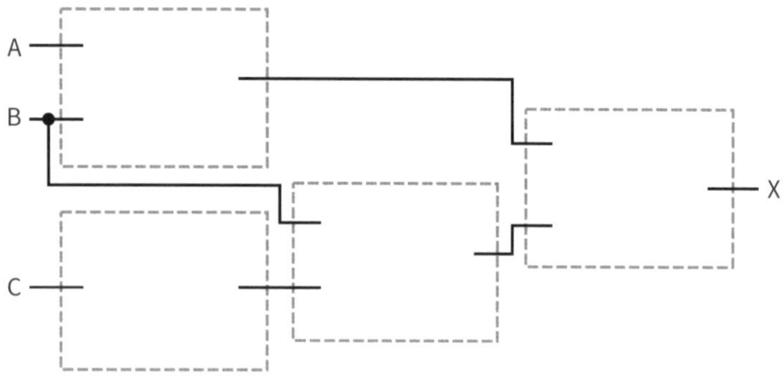

[4]

> **EXAM TIP**
>
> Some logic questions will include a scenario that will lead to a logic expression. The logic diagrams and truth tables are constructed using the same techniques as for these questions.

2 Create the truth table for the following logic diagram. **[5]**

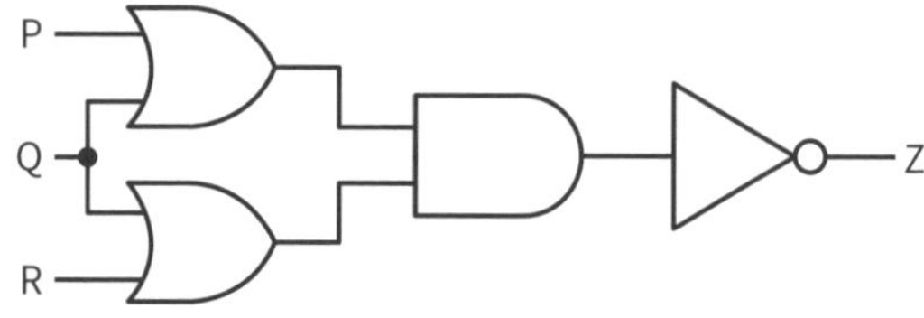

Great Clarendon Street, Oxford, OX2 6DP, United Kingdom

Oxford University Press is a department of the University of Oxford. It furthers the University's objective of excellence in research, scholarship, and education by publishing worldwide. Oxford is a registered trade mark of Oxford University Press in the UK and in certain other countries.

Written by Alison Page and David Waters

The moral rights of the authors have been asserted

First published in 2023

British Library Cataloguing in Publication Data
Data available

978-138-204408-0

10 9 8 7 6 5 4 3

The manufacturing process conforms to the environmental regulations of the country of origin.

Printed in the UK by Bell and Bain Ltd, Glasgow

Acknowledgements
The publisher and authors would like to thank the following for permission to use photographs and other copyright material:

Photos: p22: cello / Alamy Stock Photo; **p33(t):** Alexey Boldin / Shutterstock; **p33(bl):** Martin Williams / Alamy Stock Photo; **p33(br):** Neil Fraser / Alamy Stock Photo; **p37(t):** nagelestock.com / Alamy Stock Photo; **p37(m):** Kilmer Media / Alamy Stock Photo; **p37(b):** malik shah / Alamy Stock Photo; **p40(t):** sharpstock / Alamy Stock Photo; **p40(bl):** Ground Picture / Shutterstock; **p40(br):** Kilmer Media / Alamy Stock Photo; **p44:** Hennell / Alamy Stock Photo; **p53:** imageBROKER / Alamy Stock Photo; **p56(l):** Seemanta Dutta / Alamy Stock Photo; **p56(tr):** B Christopher / Alamy Stock Photo; **p56(br):** Britpix / Alamy Stock Photo; **p57:** Fascinadora / Shutterstock; **p65:** TPROduction / Shutterstock; **p70:** Juan Maria Pazos / Alamy Stock Photo; **p76:** SOPA Images Limited / Alamy Stock Photo; **p80:** Juniors Bildarchiv GmbH / Alamy Stock Photo; **p150:** Libor Vrska / Alamy Stock Photo.

Artwork by QBS Learning.

The publisher would also like to thank Adam Robbins for sharing his expertise and feedback in the development of this resource.